Europe On Purpose

The Christian Traveler's Guide

Robert H. Baylis

The Pilgrimage Press, Berkeley, California

To Naomi

CONTENTS

ILLUSTRATIONS

ACKNOWLEDGMENTS

A great many people gave invaluable assistance to this project. Dr. Ralph Winter of the World Mission Center, Pasadena, supplied technical advice and supervised the final preparations for printing. Mr. Frank Horton, Director of Emmaus Institute in Switzerland, collected a large quantity of information over several months. Rev. Christian Bastke of the Missionary Fellowship of Torchbearers gave me a number of valuable contacts and much helpful information. David and Morven Baker took time out from graduate work in London to check out various sources. Rev. and Mrs. Earl Poysti of the Pocket Testament League also provided a number of helpful contacts and Miss Cora Hogue did a valuable job of research in Italy.

My appreciation to the following who actually wrote portions of the text: Mr. David Pavey, Christian Missions in Many Lands, France; Rev. Bill Bathman of Tempe, Arizona; Brian Bounds of the Pioneers Ministry.

Dr. Donald Bloesch of Dubuque Theological Seminary very kindly referred me to sources of information about Christian communities in Europe.

Rev. John Aldis of All Souls Church, London, put me in touch with a couple of agencies without whose help the church directory in the book could not have been written.

Very helpful interviews were granted by the Rev. Michael Baughen, Rector of All Souls Church London, and the Rev. Walter Hooper of Oxford.

Thanks also go to Mr. John Todd of the B.B.C.; Rev. Harold Sloan, Secretary of the Methodist Church In Ireland; Mr. Ernie Englebert of Marburg; Dr. Manfred Siebald of the University of Mainz; Miss Ruth Siemens, Inter-Varsity staff, U.S.A.; Mr. Justin Phillips, British Information Services; Mr. Edjan Westerman of the Ichthus Fellowship, The Netherlands; Mr. Brede Kristensen, IFES director for Europe; Mr. Peter Wiegand, Director, Schloss Klaus; Mr. Wolfgang Fry, Manager, Schloss Mittersill; Mr. Richard McClelland, graduate student, Cambridge; Rev. Hans Kristian Neerskov of Mission Possible, Copenhagen; Hans Burgi, Secretary, "Mutzur Gemeinde," Switzerland; Rev. Peter Schneider, Chairman, European Evangelical Alliance; Rev. Pelle Karlsson, Philadelphia Church, Stockholm; Provst Aage Bjerno, Evangelical Alliance of Denmark; Dr. Warren Webster, Director of Conservative Baptist Foreign Missions; Dave Shaver, Assistant Director, Christian Literature Crusades; Mark Spengler, Administrator, Youth With A Mission; Rev. Jim Burroughs, Torchbearers in Southwestern France; Nelson Bezanson, Summer Program Coordinator of TEAM; Miss Karen Trana, Summer Ministries Secretary, Slavic Gospel Association; Mr. Paul Troper, U.S. Coordinator, Operation Mobilization; J.O. Blackwood, General Director, Global Outreach Mission; Bob Bingham, Director of Candidates, Overseas Christian Servicemen's Centers; Ernest C. Lubkemann, Assistant Director, Pocket Testament League; Agnes R. Hawken, Field Affairs Department, Gospel Missionary Union; David Zehr, Candidate Secretary, Greater Europe Mission; Al Young, Eastern European Bible Mission; Sam Doherty, European Director,

Child Evangelism Fellowship; Mr. Floyd McClung, Director, Dilaram Houses;
Mr. Gordon Klenck, Director of European Affairs, Campus Crusade For
Christ; Lee Howard, Foreign Missions Fellowship; Ken Shingledecker,
Director, Student Training In Missions; Kenneth M. Jones, Bible Christian
Union; Werner Burklin, European Director of Youth For Christ, International;
Dr. Jakob Nussbaumer, Director, Heimstatte Gwatt; Mr. David Burt, IFES
staff, Spain; Lyle Schrag, Wheaton College Youth Hostels Ministry.

Becky Manley of the IVCF staff was my co-leader of Summer Training Abroad
these past two years when much of this material was researched. She tolerated
my preoccupation with this project with great patience.

Important technical help was supplied by Dr. Jim Sire of the Inter-Varsity
Press, Mrs. Jackie Ormiston of J & J Travel, Walnut Creek, Don Williams of
Western Book, Oakland, and Mr. George Armerding.

Joan and Doug Anderson kept Logos-Berkeley on course during my frequent
absences, and without that kind of support the job would never have gotten done.

Finally, my thanks to Naomi who did much of the meticulous numbering to
prepare pages for the camera, and who has kept our household running
smoothly in the midst of frenzied activity for these past five months.

PREFACE

This is a book that was waiting to be written. It is a book born of the times, the Jet Age, the age when a trip to Europe for many North Americans is no more or less remarkable than a trip to the mountains or the beach was just a few years ago - - exciting, but quite commonplace. I say the book h a d to be written, because in this incredible age of mobility and speed and affluence when tens of thousands of Americans and Canadians are going to Europe, among them lots and lots of Christians, a sourcebook for giving specific directions to evangelical Christian involvement in Europe did not exist.

The idea for the book is grounded on a couple of passages from the New Testament which have also provided a framework for our Summer Training Abroad programs. They are Jesus' words in Matthew chapter 28, "Go therefore and make disciples of all nations," and those of St. Paul in 1 Corinthians 10:30, "So, whether you eat or drink, or whatever you do, do all to the glory of God." Before many of us lies the great opportunity to travel across the ocean, to walk the streets of ancient cities, to gaze upon the priceless legacy of the past. How tragically wasteful to expend so great an opportunity in ignorant and aimless wandering. How unfortunate not to gain something of more spiritual value from the journey of a lifetime than a few souvenirs and a collection of pictures of places whose significance escapes us.

It occurred to me that travel itself is nothing new for Christians. After all, most of the First Century churches were started by travelers, and making trips to the Holy Land or other sacred sites became a common practice very early in church history. It's p u r p o s e l e s s travel that is the new wrinkle, a product of our unprecedented affluence. So EUROPE ON PURPOSE is an attempt to be the antidote for that, a tool which can be put to use by the potential missionary of pilgrim alike, The book is actually addressed to t h r e e main groups - - tourists, missions candidates and students, the latter to my way of thinking having a great many advantages not open to the rest of us. But mainly, EUROPE ON PURPOSE is designed to help any Christian to "go abroad, to the glory of God."

I might say, finally, that like Pip in Charles Dickens' GREAT EXPECTA- TIONS, this book was "brought up by hand" with a minimum use of expensive equipment. This enabled me to produce it at a reasonable price, and to bring it out on a "short run" of only a few thousand copies. The two large publishers interested in this project found it economically not feasible for this reason, and also because of the need for frequent updating. Thus I have formed the Pilgrimage Press to specialize in this type of publication. I hope it will accom- plish its objectives.

Part One
The Historio-Guide

THE HISTORIO-GUIDE

The Historio-Guide is a simple teaching device based on the principle that the p a r t s of anything make more sense when one has a grasp of the w h o l e. In other words, a person can more easily understand a spark plug if he has some general idea of how an automobile ignition system works.

So it is, I believe, with sightseeing and history. Regardless of how well a guide (written or human) may explain a particular sight, say the Duomo in Florence, the tourist is never going to get a fully meaningful appreciation of it until he has some general working knowledge of the overall development of Christian civilization (and, secondarily, of the Italian Renaissance in this case).

A second principle behind the Historio-Guide is my conviction that most people are ambivalent about history. They love it if it has something to do with them or their interests, but loathe it in the abstract. Not too many high school and college students see anything relevant in the history of Western Civilization and learn just enough to get by. Thus, on the whole Americans (and probably Canadians) have a very slight grasp of European history. When they make a trip to Europe and suddenly find it relevant (as I did), their inadequate background prevents them from putting the big picture together.

The Historio-Guide does two things relative to these principles:
It gives an overview of Christian history in capsule or summary form, simple enough for the history-hater to make some sense out of it quickly;
It links the Christian sights of Europe (the parts) to the capsule history (the whole) so that anyone can appreciate any particular place or object in context.

With regard to the Guide section (B), the countries and sights within those countries are in (more or less) order of importance. This is, again, a device to try and help the visitor get the most out of a tour with the least lost motion. This kind of organization is subjective and arbitrary to a degree, and others familiar with the territory may not agree. Also, I'm sure that this first time I've left out some places that ought to be included. I'll try to amend this in future editions.

Lastly, may I hasten to point out that none of the material (or not very much anyway) is original with me, and it is in no way an attempt to be scholarly or exhaustive. I have merely taken what experts have written and put it into an easier form with the object of helping those who otherwise would not be able to appreciate the total view. For the person wishing to dig deeper, there is a bibliography which I sincerely recommend.

How the Historio-Guide works: the numbers at the side of the Guide tell you where to look for the historical context of that particular sight in the Capsule History.

SECTION A

CAPSULE HISTORY
OF
CHRISTIANITY
IN EUROPE

I The Apostolic Age

The history of Christianity in Europe began in the year 33 A.D. on a hill   A
outside the city of Jerusalem. There, according to the great historian St. Luke,
Jesus instructed His disciples, ". . .you shall be my witnesses in Jerusalem
and in all Judea and Samaria and to the end of the earth." Within a few years
there were Christian congregations throughout the Mediterranean world, giving
evidence that this command had been literally carried out.

The first Christian mission to Europe was accomplished around the year
50 A.D. when the Apostle Paul, accompanied by Silas, Timothy and Luke himself, crossed the narrow straits between Troas (a Turkish town call Troia still
exists near the site) and the port of Samothrace in the Roman province of
Macedonia. The colony of Philippi was the first European city to hear the Gospel
from the lips of Paul, followed by Thessalonica, Beroea, Athens and Corinth.
Later (about 61 A.D.) Paul reached Rome itself, but as a prisoner. Possibly he
was able to complete an anticipated journey to Spain before being rearrested and
executed around 64 A.D. during the persecution launched by Nero.

The Apostle Peter, in the meanwhile, was engaged in preaching the Gospel
to Jews and in establishing the church among Hebrew converts in Asia Minor.
Evidence exists that he reached Rome later in his career and was executed
there around the same time as Paul.

The modern traveler can find three types of landmarks in Europe dating   B
from the ancient world and the 1st century A.D. that have significance from a
Christian historical perspective. First are the pagan monuments, usually of a
religious nature, some of which date to as early as 2000 B.C. Second, there are
the Roman remains to be found extensively in England, France, Germany,
Switzerland and all along the northern Mediterranean. Not all are as early as
the Apostolic Age, of course, but their associations with the beginnings of
Christianity make them of particular interest. The third type belong to the first
two catagories as well, but have added significance because of their association
with the apostles or the 1st century church. The catacombs near Rome would be
an example.

II The Roman Period

During the 500 year period between the death of the last apostle and the be- A
ginning of the Middle Ages, the primary tangible legacy left to us by the
Christian church are documents. During the early years Christians did not have
special buildings and for the most part were a persecuted people. The earliest
Christian buildings now left to us are the following: the 5th century Church of
St. Demetrius in Salonika (Greece), and Sant' Apollinare In Classe (534-538),
Sant' Apollinare Nuovo (c. 500), Basilica Ursiana (370-380) and San Vitale (547),
all in Ravenna, Italy.

The early church was beset with internal struggles with various heresies, and externally with periodic crackdowns by the Roman government, often accompanied by severe violence. As part of their efforts to preserve the truth of the Gospel, the church fathers settled the question of which books to include in the Biblical canon, and from time to time met to formulate creeds (or doctrinal statements). Along with the preservation of Biblical truth, however, a body of church traditions grew up which most Protestants feel cannot be substantiated by Scripture. These include the authority of the bishops of Rome and Constantinople (i.e., the pope and the Greek Orthodox patriarch), the sanctity of church buildings, the veneration of images and the exclusive power of a priest to administer the sacraments.

CONSTANTINE THE GREAT

B   A most notable development in Christian history came at the beginning of the fourth century. Constantine, heir apparent to the throne of the Roman Empire, emerged triumphant from a battle with his rival, Maxentius, in A.D. 312. He claimed to have seen a vision of the cross before the battle and adopted this as his standard. Constantine, subsequently, in the Edict of Milan (313) granted full legal toleration for Christianity. He became involved personally in trying to resolve some of the differences between Christians, summoned the Council of Nicea in 325 and influenced the creed that resulted. In 330 he founded a capital for Christianity in the eastern part of the empire at Byzantium, which he called Constantinople. This was the beginning of the Byzantine period in church art (though it had earlier roots), and of the Eastern Orthodox Church. The Great Schism marking the official separation of the Eastern Orthodox from the Roman Catholic Church occurred in 1054. The eastern parts of the Orthodox church did not experience the Protestant Reformation, and it has just been in recent years that the evangelical spirit has penetrated its domains. Constantinople itself fell to the Turks in 1453, but the Patriarch kept his office in that city.

THE FOURTH TO SIXTH CENTURIES

C   The 4th century was marked by bitter theological controversies on the one hand and by the emergence of some of the greatest figures in church history on the other. These included Augustine of Hippo (author of THE CITY OF GOD), John Chrysostrom (whose writings on Christian morality were especially appreciated by the 16th century Reformers) and Jerome (who is responsible for the Latin Vulgate version of the Bible, the only Bible widely used until the 16th century). In 410 the last of the Roman legions left Britain and the pagan Angles, Saxons and Jutes poured across the Channel and destroyed the church which had been established under the Romans in eastern England and southeastern Scotland. The Celtic church continued its life in western Britain and Ireland. Finally Rome itself fell in 476. The bishop of Rome retained his power, however, and Christianity, often in a weak condition and buffeted by heresy and controversy, lived on as Europe became fragmented into numerous barbarian states.

III The Middle Ages

The Middle Ages is the name given to the seven hundred year period in   A
Europe between the offices of Popes Gregory I and (roughly) that of Boniface VIII.
Gregory was the chief architect of the papal system that dominated western civ-
ilization for many centuries. He claimed universal supremacy in the church and
took upon himself the title of Vicar of Christ On Earth. (And, incidentally, gave
his name to the form of church music called the Gregorian Chant.) During
Gregory's office the traditions of the Roman Catholic Church, which had appeared as early as the 2nd and 3rd centuries, now became established practice.
These included, in addition to papal claims to supremacy, belief in the real
Presence of Christ in the mass, in Purgatory, in prayers to saints and in Mary
as the "Mother of God." Altars, previously associated with pagan religions, became part of church furnishings, and the churches themselves became more
elaborate. Priests emerged as a separate caste, endowed with mystical powers
and removed from the people.

EARLY MISSIONARY ACTIVITY

During the Middle Ages Christianity spread from Rome to Saxon Britain,   B
and from Celtic Britain to Europe. Augustine, sent by Gregory in 596, made
his headquarters in Canterbury, and the religious life of England has been associated with this town and its great cathedral ever since. The church in Scotland
and Ireland, however, had remained since Roman times. Patrick had come to
Ireland in 432 and the Gospel had flourished. Even earlier St. Ninian had built
a church and monastery on Scotland's Solway Firth in 397 and evangelized the
northern regions of Britain. The great St. Columba went from Ireland to the island of Iona in 503 and Aidan went from Iona to the island of Lindisfarne in 635.
From here the Gospel was carried to Northern England as well as to Scotland.
About twenty years after Columba reached Iona, missionaries went out to the
Continent of Europe from the Celtic church at Bangor, Ireland. Churches and
monasteries were established in Central Europe as far as Hungary. Later in
the century two great Englishmen, Willibrord from York and Boniface from
Devon, did a vast work of evangelization among the Germanic tribes as repre-
sentatives of the Roman church.

CHRISTIANITY IN ENGLAND 664-1066

The two forms of Christianity in the British Isles, Irish (or Celtic) and   C
Roman Catholic, gradually merged in favor of the latter after the king of the
Northumbrians decided in favor of the Catholics at the Synod of Whitby in 664.
Anglo-Saxon England was divided into seven kingdoms (called The Heptarchy)
which developed out of the tribal system of the invading peoples. The greatest
of these little kingdoms was that of Wessex (now known generally as the West
Country), whose king, Alfred (870-899) was the ablest and best educated of the
Saxon rulers. Alfred was a devout and intelligent Christian, and brought into

being a renaissance equal in importance to that of Charlemagne in Germany. He translated the ECCLESIASTICAL HISTORY OF THE ENGLISH PEOPLE of England's first great Christian writer, The Venerable Bede (673-735). Through Bede we learn of Caedmon, an illiterate stable keeper who was given a divine gift of composing verses (or poems) on the Scriptures.

Alfred, together with other scholars he had gathered around him at his capital at Winchester, translated other great works such as Pope Gregory's PASTORAL CARE, the Christian poems ascribed to Cynewulf, bishop of Lindisfarne (d. 783) and the most famous of all of England's early poems, BEOWULF. Alfred also inaugurated the ANGLO-SAXON CHRONICLE, which recorded English history from the dim past to his own day, and which was continued by monks after his death. Alfred beat back the pagan Danes who had occupied the north and east and preserved unity among the central Anglo-Saxon nations.

After Alfred's death, however, Anglo-Saxon culture began to disintegrate under the siege of the invaders. It was finally merged with that of the Normans after the conquest in 1066. A few remains of Saxon monastic and church architecture can be seen here and there, and the ANGLO-SAXON CHRONICLE rests in the British Museum. The memory of Alfred and the kingdom that he created is preserved at Winchester.

CHARLEMAGNE AND THE CAROLINGIAN DYNASTY

D   Charlemagne, king of the Franks (North Germans), was the grandson of the great hero Charles Martel who drove back the invading Muslim armies at the Battle of Tours (732). Charlemagne conquored all of Central Europe in the late 8th and early 9th centuries. Like his father Pepin the Short, Charlemagne defended the Pope against his enemies, and in turn was rewarded by being crowned emperor of the Holy Roman Empire on Christmas Day, 800. This gave rise to the papal claim that the glories of the ancient Roman Empire had been revived. The alliance of one state, one church, worked well in this instance because Charlemagne was a capable administrator and morally upright. Moreover, he maintained his position of emperor over the pontiff. Charlemagne attempted to lay down regulations bearing on the moral lives of the clergy. He encouraged learning, and his new capital at Aachen was a gathering place for scholars from all over Europe.

Charlemagne's successors did not inherit his capabilities, however, and his reign was followed by a period of great political disorder in the church and chaos in the government of the empire. Muslim armies from Africa took possession of Sicily and Southern Italy, Hungarian Magyars threatened from the east and lawlessness became the norm throughout Europe. The last member of the Carolingian house, Charles the Fat, was deposed in 887.

THE HOLY GERMANIC EMPIRE AND THE END OF THE DARK AGES

E   After the fall of the Carolingian dynasty, the Italian nobles of Tuscany acquired control of Rome and the papacy became prey to avarice, intrigue and immorality. Three beautiful but unscrupulous women, Theodora and her two daughters Marozia and Theodora, for a time filled the papal chair with their paramours and illegitimate children. In 960 Pope John XII appealed to Otto I, king of Germany, for help against Berenger II of Italy, and out of this alliance came a new empire somewhat smaller than that of Charlemagne called The Holy Germanic Empire. Like Charlemagne, Otto was a strong monarch and later deposed John on charges of murder, blasphemy and gross sensuality. Otto's reign marked the turning point of the great decline of civilization in Europe following the fall of the Roman Empire often called The Dark Ages, and brought about the establishment of feudalism and the manorial system.

FEUDALISM AND LIFE ON A MEDIEVAL MANOR

Feudalism was an organization of the ruling class in an agrarian society in F which values were reckoned in terms of personal service. Feudal lords and feudal vassals were bound to one another by service, and the military service which a vassal owed his lord was of supreme importance. Great lords were vassels to greater lords, and in a sense all of Europe was interrelated in this way during the Middle Ages - - except for the church. The vassel swore that he would be faithful to his lord and the lord conferred a fief, or gift of lands, upon the vassel, symbolized by giving him some token (a lance, glove, etc.) of his protection. This ceremony was called investiture, and it was valid for life, thus binding lord and vassel in a compact of interdependence.

The manorial system is the name given to the agrarian organization of Medieval society. The feudal lords lived in fortified dwellings in the midst of their lands, and those lands were worked by serfs who were paid by a share of what the lands produced. The manor was the only world the serf knew. Each manor had its priest and comprised a parish, and all the the peasants received of Christian truth came through that source. Inasfar as even the priests were often illiterate, it is safe to assume that even though the church and the Christian religion dominated all of society, the individual was fairly ignorant of the Word of God. On the other hand, there was without doubt here and there a parish priest who, like Chaucer's Parson, not only taught the people the Gospel but "folwed it hymselve."

THE NORSE PIRATES

During the period of misgovernment in the 9th century following the reign   G of Charlemagne, Norse pirates (often called Vikings) repeatedly attacked the coasts of Europe, and even advanced inland along the Rhine Valley. So vicious was their style of warfare and so ruthless their policy of destroying everything that was not looked upon by them as booty that the advances of civilization brought about by Charlemagne were very nearly wiped out. For a time they threatened to submerge Europe in barbarism once again, but finally (and amazingly) they became Christian and settled in Normandy. In 1066, under William the Conqueror, they successfully invaded and subjugated England.

THE SPREAD OF CHRISTIANITY IN EUROPE 800-1300

Early in the 9th century Ansgar, the "Apostle to the North," carried the Gos- H pel to Denmark and Norway, but all Scandinavia did not become Christian until late in the 11th century. Moravia and Bulgaria became outwardly Christian in the mid-9th century under the swords of their rulers. In Bohemia, some of the princes were converted, but the people resisted Christianity because it came to them from German sources. Poland became nominally Christian in 968, the Hungarian Magyars came under the Christian influence from 973 onward through the work of Piligrim, and Russia received the Gospel in 988 through emmissaries from Constantinople. In later years it became one of the great bulwarks of the Orthodox church. By the end of the 13th century, at least nominal Christianity covered all of Europe except Finland and Lapland.

THE MONASTIC SYSTEM

I   Monasticism, the forming of celibate communities for the purpose of living more wholly for God, appeared first in the eastern parts of the Roman Empire. St. Martin of Tours (France) was one of the first monastic leaders in Europe, and his work greatly influenced St. Ninian later in the 4th century. The early Celtic church was monastic in its organization. Later Roman Catholic monastic orders were:

The Benedictines, founded in 529 by St. Benedict at Monte Cassino (Italy)

The Cluniac Movement, started by Bernon in 910

The Cistercians, founded at Citeaux in Burgundy, whose most famous abbot was St. Bernard who established the monastery of Clairvaux in 1115

The Franciscans, founded by St. Francis of Assisi in 1209

The Dominicans, started in 1215 by Dominic, a Spanish nobleman. To this order the pope committed the vicious engine of the Inquisition.

The Knights of St. John, the Knights Templars and the Teutonic Knights, founded during the Crusades as military orders

REFORM AND THE RISE OF PAPAL POWER

J   The great organization of the Cluniac Movement with over 300 monasteries was built around the idea of being free from lay control and answerable to the Pope alone. Each abbey chose its own abbot. The movement initiated much needed reform among the clergy. A young monk, Hildebrand, who had been advisor to the popes, became himself Pope Gregory VII in 1073. Following Cluniac teachings, he objected strongly to all secular interference in church affairs and defied the German emperor, Henry IV. Henry retaliated by marching on Rome and it was necessary for Gregory to take refuge in the Castle of St. Angelo. However, the forces set in motion by Gregory eventually brought the papacy to the height of its power in the 12th and 13th centuries. Innocent III, who ascended the papal throne in 1198, brought both Philip of France and John of England to their knees, and his political power extended in one way or another over almost all Christian lands. He launched the Third Crusade, and waged full scale war against what he regarded as heresy. His magnificence reached its zenith in the splendor of the Lateran Council of 1215, one of the greatest Ecumenical Councils of all time.

THE CRUSADES 1095-1270

The idea of a Crusade to rescue Jerusalem from the Muslims was espoused K
by Hildebrand and later carried out by his successors. The First Crusade,
which took place in 1095, was strongly supported by Pope Urban II, who recognized the prestige that leadership in a popular campaign of this sort would bring
to the papacy. One method of gaining volunteers was the granting of indulgences
- - absolution from sins, cancellation of debts, pardon for criminals, etc. - -
on the part of the pope.

The first official Crusade was preceded by an unofficial expedition led by
Peter the Hermit, which ended in disaster. The official campaign, some 300,000
strong, which set out in August, was plagued by many hardships. Tens of thousands perished on the way. There was also conflict within the leadership. They
reached Jerusalem in 1099 and took the city after a siege.

In all there were eight Crusades, but only the first achieved what it set out
to do. The Second Crusade was organized by Bernard of Clairvaux when the
Turks captured Edessa in 1144. It ended in defeat. The re-capture of Jerusalem
by Saladin in 1187 resulted in the Third Crusade, led by the emperor Frederick
Barbarossa of the Holy Roman Empire, Philip of France and Richard the Lion-
hearted of England. Barbarossa was drowned and Richard and Philip, in spite of
amazing heroism, virtually failed. The Fourth and Sixth Crusades, though somewhat successful, did not have papal recognition. The Fifth, Seventh and Eighth
were all failures.

MONASTERIES AND CATHEDRALS

The great period of monastery building occurred in the 11th and 12th cen-   L
turies, and the style of architecture used is called Romanesque. This was
followed in the 12th and 13th centuries by the great period of cathedral building,
reflecting the shift of episcopal centers from rural monasteries to the towns
then just coming into existence. The style of cathedral architecture of this time
is called Gothic. Many examples both of monastic churches and other struc -
tures, and of cathedrals can be seen throughout Europe. In general, however,
cathedrals have been more successful than monasteries in surviving the ra-
vages of time, war and politics. The latter are often found as beautiful ruins.

A visit to a cathedral can be a highly rewarding experience for the Christian traveler. Everything has spiritual meaning - - the great tower often topped
by a spire, the carved stone facade, the stained glass, the ancient effigies of
kings, nobles, famous churchmen and, occasionally, humble servants of God,
the various pieces of furniture, even the shape of the building itself. Gothic
cathedrals are in the shape of a cross, with the foot (the nave) facing westward.
They were built on the principle of vaults and arches, and the impression of
height often strikes the visitor first of all. The very best of Medieval crafts-
manship went into the building and furnishings of the cathedral and the sight,
say, of sunlight streaming through the jewel-like glass or of an intricately
carved stone screen is breathtaking. Cathedrals are generally divided into
three main parts - - the nave where the laity gather for various services, the
choir (behind a screen east of the transcepts or cross arms of the building)

where the clergy sit in the stalls to hear sermons, and where music is performed, and the sanctuary at the east end where the high altar is located.

When visiting a cathedral, it is always wise to purchase a guide book. A
group planning to visit an English cathedral can write ahead and secure the
services of a verger, who will give a tour of an hour or so for no charge.

ILLUMINATED MANUSCRIPTS OF THE MIDDLE AGES

M   Manuscript illumination is an art form peculiar to the Middle Ages, and is
of particular interest to the Christian because illumination, or embellishment
in color and gold, is directly associated with the production and preservation
of the Bible during that period. Fine European illuminated manuscript Bibles
appeared as early as the 6th century, but the art flowered during the time of
Charlemagne. By the 15th century, when printing was invented, illumination
was more imitative than creative and hand produced books no longer met the
needs of the time. The first printed book, the Gutenburg Bible, however, retained hand done embellishment and in many ways was an imitation of the illuminated manuscript. Fine examples of illuminated manuscripts may be seen at:

     the Library of Trinity College, Dublin (Book of Kells, 9th century)
     the British Museum (Lindisfarne Gospels)
     the Bibliothéque Nationale, Paris
     the Vatican Library, Rome
     the Laurentian Library, Florence
     the Abbey Library, St. Gallen, Switzerland
     the Biblioteca Nacional, Madrid

MYSTERY PLAYS

N   Mystery or Miracle Plays, which were produced by the Medieval church
and later by trade guilds, apparently had their origin in little dramas per -
formed by the clergy at Christmas and Easter. By the 14th century the guilds
had developed Biblical dramas appropriate to each trade, which were presented
in the center of town on stages built on wagons. Thus the shipwrights would present THE BUILDING OF THE ARK, the fishermen would give NOAH AND THE
FLOOD, the bakers THE LAST SUPPER, etc. Characters developed into stereo-
types, such as the shrew (Noah's wife), the tyrant (Herod), and so on. Comedy
was introduced, sometimes by way of sub-plots, such as the theft of a sheep
during THE BIRTH OF CHRIST. In the 14th century the Morality Play also
appeared. This generally was some sort of contest between Good and Evil.
EVERYMAN is the most celebrated on the Morality Plays. It is produced
annually in Salzburg, Austria, during the Mozart Festival. Miracle Plays are
staged every several years in the old city of York in England.

IV The Decline of the Medieval Church

The papacy began to weaken during the days of Boniface VIII (1294-1304),   A
who arrogantly insisted that all temporal rulers were subject to him (and that
subjectivity to the Pope was necessary for salvation). This led to conflicts with
Edward I of England and Philip the Fair of France. In the end Boniface was arrested through the agency of Philip and so roughly treated that he died. The
next pope, Clement V, was so much under Philip's control that he could not face
the indignation of the Italian people, and removed to France. For seventy years
the popes resided in Avignon, France, a period called the "Babylonish Captivity"
by some Catholic historians. Gregory XI returned to Rome in 1377.

When Gregory died, the Italian cardinals elected Urban VI and the French
cardinals elected Clement VII. Thus began a schism that lasted nearly forty
years. Some nations supported the French pope and others the Italian, and the
two sides each claimed to be the true successor of Peter's chair and heaped an-
athama upon one another.

EARLY OPPOSITION TO CATHOLIC DOCTRINE

Christian bodies outside the Roman Catholic Church had appeared as early B
as the 7th century. From the end of the 12th century a sect called the Beghards
flourished in the Netherlands and along the Rhine. The best known of these
groups are the Waldenses, followers of Peter Waldo, who spread throughout
Europe but were most numerous in Medieval times in the Alpine regions and
northern Italy (where congregations exist to this day). These people rejected the
worldly structure of the Catholic system and based their faith and practices on
the teachings of Scripture. They posed a threat to the unity of the organized
church and were severely persecuted. In one infamous instance an army insti-
gated by Pope Innocent III massacred a heretical sect called the Albigenses in
1208 and killed many of the Waldenses as well.

JOHN WYCLIF AND JOHN HUS

In the 14th century, voices of protest also began to be heard from within the C
Catholic Church on the issue of Biblical versus Church authority. Marsilius of
Padua, a physician, and a leading Franciscan scholar at the University of Paris,
William of Occam, were among these. The most influential of the radical
churchmen, however, were John Wyclif (or Wycliffe) in England (1320-1384) and
John Hus in Bohemia (1360-1415). Wyclif was one of the ablest scholars at Oxford
University. He declared that "the only head of the church is Christ," and he or-
ganized bands of priests (nicknamed Lollards) who preached the Word to the
common people. To facilitate this ministry, his followers translated the Latin

Vulgate Bible into the English of the time, producing in manuscript form the first complete English Bible. Hus, born a peasant, rose to become Rector of Prague University, the most important learning center in Europe after Paris and Oxford. He was genuinely converted and became a powerful preacher of the Gospel in the Bohemian language. Being deeply influenced by the teachings of Wyclif, he fearlessly rebuked the clergy for their vices.

V The Renaissance

A   The Renaissance (the word means "rebirth") is the name given to a period in Europe from the 14th through the 16th centuries when the Medieval church and the Medieval way of life lost its control over the minds and lives of the people, to be replaced by new learning, new artistic expression, new personal freedom and the beginnings of modern society. Education and learning in the Middle Ages was dominated by the Roman church, which was in turn dominated by Scholasticism. This was a system of philosophy and theology which rested more on the opinions of the church fathers, particularly Thomas Aquinas, than on the Bible. Scholasticism had "all the answers" - - there was no room for new ideas. Christians (and others) who deviated were ruthlessly persecuted, as has been noted earlier.

B   The Renaissance came to Europe through a rediscovery of ancient Greek and Roman writings which were translated from Arabic manuscripts brought from the east. Other eastern contributions, such as gunpowder and the compass, also played an important part. In these ancient writings the thinkers of the day found radical ideas that were in direct opposition to Scholasticism. In the 14th century, certain Italian writers such as Dante (THE DIVINE COMEDY), Petrarch (SONNETS) and Boccaccio (THE DECAMERON) expressed in popular form and in the vernacular language a break-away from tradition. At the same time they passionately pursued a study of the ancient classics. The great English writer, Geoffrey Chaucer, who visited Italy and was highly influenced by Boccaccio, wrote the Middle English classic THE CANTERBURY TALES during this century. In these story poems, supposedly told by a group of pilgrims on the way to Thomas Becket's shrine at Canterbury Cathedral, a wide cross section of people including several in religious orders reveal the secular spirit of the age and the dissipated state of the Medieval church.

ISLAM

In tracing the course of European Christian civilization it is impossible to   C
ignore Islam. Traces of the conflict between the Christians and the invading
Muslim armies can still be seen in many parts of Europe. Mohammad was born
in Mecca, in Arabia, around 570. He wrote the Koran, the sacred book of the
Muslims, around 610, not long after the death of Gregory I. By 712 the Islamic
armies had conquered North Africa, the Middle East, India and Spain. They
pushed across the Pyrenees, but were stopped at Tours in 732 by Christian
forces under Charles Martel in one of the important battles of all history.
Ironically, some of the greatest advances in Western Civilization (mathematics,
for example) came from the Muslim world. Thus in a sense the Renaissance
exploded upon Europe through the catalyst created by Islam.

THE INVENTION OF PRINTING

From a Christian as well as a secular point of view, the greatest invention D
in modern world history is that of printing. To a combination of materials and
processes known earlier (e. g., ink, paper, the press, the codex or "book" as
opposed to scrolls), Johann Gutenberg of Mainz, Germany, added the technique
of movable type (that is, setting type from individual metal letters), and in 1455
produced a beautiful edition of the Latin Bible. Printing quickly spread throughout Europe, and by 1500 at least one thousand printers were in business. Thus
it was possible for the New Learning to spread rapidly and for people to form
independent opinions of great works of literature, particularly the Bible.
During the infancy of printing before 1500, at least 100 different editions of the
Latin Bible had been printed. Appropriately, there is today a museum of
printing in Mainz, located near the site of Gutenberg's shop, and the treasure
of the collection is one of the few 42-line Gutenberg Bibles still in existence.

RENAISSANCE ART

The Renaissance is perhaps best known for its great art, which flourished   E
first in the northern Italian cities of Florence, Venice and Rome. The magnificent cathedral of Florence designed by Filippo Brunelleschi and the Cathedral
of St. Peter's in Rome planned by Bramante and Michaelangelo are outstanding
examples of architecture. The paintings of Giotto, Masaccio, Perugino,
Mantegna, daVinci, Raphael, Michaelangelo, Bellini, Giorgione, Titian,
Tintoretto, Fra Lippo Lippi, Fra Angelico, Botticelli (next to daVinci and
Michaelangelo, the greatest of the Florentines) and Paolo Veronese are among
the world's most famous. They can be seen in many museums throughout
Europe, but principally in Florence (some 27 universities have art schools in
Florence). The Renaissance also produced some great artists in the north of
Europe, notably the brothers Van Eyck in Flanders, Albrecht Durer in Ger-
many and Hans Holbein the Younger in England. Among sculptors, Michael-
angelo stands supreme; his DAVID, MOSES and THE PIETA are without peer.
Michaelangelo also produced the world's greatest wall paintings, in the Cistine
Chapel of the Vatican, rivaled only by daVinci's LAST SUPPER.

THE HUMANISTS

F   A term generally given to the classical scholars of the Renaissance is Humanist, meaning that these men were interested in the pursuit of knowledge about this world (as opposed to the other-worldly view of the Scholastics. Thus we can identify as Humanists Dante, Petrarch and Boccaccio (mentioned earlier) and also later literary figures such as Machiavelli (THE PRINCE), Spencer of England (THE FAERIE QUEENE), Cervantes of Spain (DON QUIXOTE) and Montaigne of France (ESSAYS).

It is a mistake to confuse the Renaissance Humanists with the present day use of the term Humanist, which generally denotes a philosophy at odds with the Christian world view. The Renaissance Humanists were men of courage and ideals, and all of them contributed something of worth to the world's store of knowledge as they struck out, not against the truth of Christianity, but against the ignorance, superstition and vice perpetuated by the backward system of the Medieval church. Three outstanding Humanists were actually members of the clergy and committed Christians.

Savonarola (1452-1498) was an earnest, saintly man who profoundly influenced many of the intellectuals of his day as he preached against worldliness in the church. He aimed at making Florence a theocratic republic, but was unjustly charged with heresy and cruelly executed. John Colet (1466-1519) was one of a group of brilliant scholars who came under the influence of Savonarola. Colet rejected Scholasticism, and became famous for his lectures on the Epistles of St. Paul. As Dean of St. Paul's Cathedral in London, he attacked the immoral lives of the clergy and called for the bishops to reform. William Tyndale was one of his pupils, as was Desiderius Erasmus.

Desiderius Erasmus (1467-1536), often called Erasmus of Rotterdam, is generally acclaimed as the greatest Humanist of all. For a short time he was professor of Divinity and Greek at Cambridge University. His writings include two books, IN PRAISE OF FOLLY and COLLOQUIES, that castigate the monastic system with biting satire and which were banned by the Roman Catholic Church. Erasmus produced the first printed Greek New Testament, sometimes called "textus abomnibus receptus" (the universally received text) as it was the basis for all English translations of the New Testament, including the King James Version, until the late 19th century. Erasmus, though bitterly hated by the monks and many of the Catholic clergy, remained within the church as did Savonarola and Colet.

VI The Reformation

The evangelical Protestant church as we know it today, with its many de-   A
nominations, diverse forms of organization and worship and heavy emphasis
upon the use of the vernacular Bible, was born in the 16th and 17th centuries
through a movement (or perhaps, more accurately, a process) called the
Protestant Reformation. During this period the various revolutionary changes
in society, in the arts and learning and in the realm of faith, which had been
building up pressure over some two centuries, combined with a wave of genuine
spiritual conviction throughout Europe and broke against the Roman Catholic
bulwarks of tradition. Almost everywhere Catholicism was engulfed and Protestant churches arose (some to stand, others to be re-engulfed in the Counter-
Reformation that followed). In general, there were four types of Protestant
movements, and some knowledge of their origins is vital to understanding the
Christian church in Europe today.

MARTIN LUTHER AND THE LUTHERAN CHURCH

The Protestant Reformation was not directly a by-product of the Renais-   B
sance, although the Renaissance prepared the ground by making it possible for
scholars to get back beyond the Latin Vulgate Bible of Jerome to the Greek and
Hebrew texts, and by making the Bible generally more available. The Reformation, like so many great movements, began with a single man. The man in
this case was Martin Luther. Luther, a young German law student, suddenly
left the university for an Augustinian convent in 1505. Unable to find peace with
God through confession and penance, he discovered a Latin Bible and through
reading the EPISTLE TO THE ROMANS entered into a personal relationship
with Jesus Christ. Some years later, in preparing lectures in ROMANS for
theological students at the University of Wittenburg, Luther came to a full
realization of the meaning of the Pauline doctrine of justification by faith.

Ironically, the building of the great Renaissance church of St. Peter's in   C
Rome helped to trigger Luther's revolt. Pope Leo X needed large sums of
money for this project and decided to raise the funds by extending the sale of
indulgences (see Crusades). Tetzel, a Dominican monk, shamelessly hawked
the indulgences near Wittenburg and Luther, stirred to the depths, wrote his
celebrated Ninety-Five Theses (or objections to the indulgences). On All Saints
Day, 1517, he nailed them to the church door at Wittenburg where great crowds
gathered. The Latin theses were translated, and copies were printed and distributed all over Germany. Because he gave expression to what was in the
hearts of many people, Luther soon became famous.

Having ignored the pope's summons to Rome, Luther was questioned by   D
Cardinal Cajetan, the papal legate, at Augsburg. Luther refused to recant. In
1519, in a debate at Leipsig involving the papal champion John Eck, Luther

declared that the supremacy of the pope was unknown in Scripture. From here on Luther clearly understood that he had severed himself from the authority of the Roman church and began to defend his cause by a stream of printed sermons and pamphlets. A young professor of Greek, Malanchthon, became his companion and lifelong friend, complementing with calmness Luther's fiery personality during his lifetime and becoming his successor at his death.

E   In 1520 Luther circulated his three most famous pamphlets, TO THE CHRISTIAN NOBILITY OF THE GERMAN NATION, CONCERNING THE FREEDOM OF A CHRISTIAN MAN and ON THE BABYLONIAN CAPTIVITY OF THE CHURCH. He received the papal bull of excommunication with orders to burn his works in June of that year. Arrayed in the robes of his order before a great crowd outside Wittenburg, Luther flung the bull, the Canon Law and a copy of the Decretals (ancient documents affirming the power of the pope, which he had discovered were forged) onto a huge bonfire.

F   Luther's next major confrontation was at Worms in 1521. The young Charles V, new head of the Holy Roman Empire which included Spain, part of Germany and a large section of Eastern Europe, was hesitant to surpress the Reformers by force because he needed their help against the Muslims. He called the Diet of Worms to which a great company of princes and nobles were invited, in order to put down Luther peacably. Luther refused to retract any of his writings, however, and ended his defense with the famous declaration, "Here I stand. I can do no other. So help me God. Amen."

G   On the way back to Wittenburg Luther was captured by a troop of horsemen sent by the Elector of Saxony, who feared for his safety, and conducted to the castle of the Wartburg where he was confined for nearly a year. While his enemies thought he had perished, Luther was busy translating the New Testament from Greek into German, a work of supreme importance in the Reformation.

Luther returned to Wittenburg in 1522 and resumed leadership of his movement at a time when it began to be dominated by extremists. In 1526 Charles V called another Diet, this time at Speier, again with the hope of suppressing the followers of Luther. However, the Diet issued an edict declaring that each state in Germany be allowed to hold the religion of its ruling prince. This was finally accepted at the Peace of Augsburg in 1555. Another Diet of Speier in 1529 declared that the German states following Reformed teaching should remain so. But that the other states should remain Catholic with no opportunity to introduce Reformed doctrine. The evangelical members of the Diet protested this ruling - - hence the name "Protestant." Thereafter, the German Catholics formed a Catholic League to protect their interests and the Protestant princes such as the Elector of Saxony and the Landgrave of Hesse organized the League of Schmalkald. Thus Germany was divided into Protestant and Catholic sections bitterly opposed to one another.

H   Martin Luther was one of the greatest figures in the annals of the Christian church. His legacy to the whole church is extensive: his hymns (notably A MIGHTY FORTRESS IS OUR GOD), his translation of the Bible into German, his commentaries on the Scriptures, etc. But, being human, he made errors which created problems later on. In 1525 he urged the authorities to crush a

revolt of the peasants unmercifully, thus alienating many supporters. In 1529
the Landgrave of Hesse arranged for a meeting of the German and Swiss
Reformers at his castle at Marburg. This meeting is called the Marburg
Colloquy. Luther stubbornly refused to compromise with Zwingli and the other
Swiss brethren on the question of the eucharist - - he insisted that the real
Presence of Christ was in the elements, though they were not a means of grace.
Thereafter there was no reconciliation between the two bodies of Christians.
Finally, in the opinion of many (but not all) evangelicals, Luther retained too
many of the Roman Catholic elements in the churches that bear his name,
including the crucifix, candles and Mass vestments.

* * * * *

THE ANABAPTISTS

The name Anabaptist came into being during the beginnings of the Refor-   I
mation and referred to Christians who objected to infant baptism and rebap-
tized those who joined their communion. The term was one of derision, given
by members of established churches to those who were regarded as radicals
and heretics. There was some justification for this opinion. In 1522, during
Luther's absence, a preacher named Storch with other self-styled "prophets"
from Zwickau caused great excitement in Wittenburg. An associate of Storch,
one Thomas Munzer, helped to fire the peasant's revolt of 1524 by his wild
preaching that the Millenium was about to take place. The worst example of
fanatical excess took place in Munster, Germany, in the years 1533-35. Led by
a former Lutheran minister, Bernard Rothmann, and a Dutch prophet named
John of Leyden, the city set itself up as the New Zion with John of Leyden as
king. They believed it their duty to exterminate the ungodly and a proclamation
to this effect was circulated in the Netherlands. A band of men and women ran
naked through the streets of Amsterdam shouting "Woe, woe, the wrath of God
falls on this city!" Later the city hall of Amsterdam was attacked. Finally, in
June, 1535, Munster was re-captured and the extremists put to death. Even
today many European Christians think of Anabaptists as wild eyed fanatics.

A re-examination of the facts in recent years has led to the conclusion by   J
many scholars that most Anabaptists were devout believers who refused to
recognize infant baptism, held that the church should be separate from the
state and put great stress on the study of the Scriptures. Generally, the groups
developed in four parts of Europe. First was the Swiss group founded by Conrad
Grebel and Felix Manz at Zurich in 1522. Grebel and Manz were former pupils
of the Reformer Zwingli, and both along with many others were put to death for
their beliefs. The second group appeared in South Germany and were led at first
by Balthasar Hubmaier and Hans Denk, and after their martyrdom by Pilgrim
Marbeck. The third group was led by Jacob Hutter in Moravia until his execution in 1536, and became distinguished for their practice of communal life.
Later, they became known as the Hutterites, and have done prominent work in
many countries including Russia, Canada and the United States. A few communities still exist. Another group which came to practice the communal life were
the Mennonites, followers of the Dutch Anabaptist Menno Simons. The
Mennonites had many struggles with their conviction that they should form a

pure body of saints apart from the world. While most Mennonites take their place among evangelical Protestants today, being particularly known for their pacifism and community service, the extreme interpretation of this conviction can be seen in the Amish communities of Pennsylvania.

* * * * *

THE REFORMED CHURCH

K   The Reformed Church is the official church today in most of Switzerland, in Holland and in Scotland (where it is called the Presbyterian Church), and has a great many congregations in the United States and the British Commonwealth. The Puritans of the late 16th and early 17th centuries were part of the Reformed Church movement.

L   The Reformed Church had its beginnings in Zurich, Switzerland under Ulrich Zwingli, the minister of the great cathedral church. Switzerland is the oldest democracy in the world, and this may have something to do with the characteristically democratic form of Reformed Church government. Zwingli took his stand on the Word of God and denounced the unbiblical doctrines of the Roman Catholic Church. The city council of Zurich set up an independent church in 1522, and Reformed doctrines spread to Berne, Basel and other Swiss cities. However, the forest cantons remained Catholic, and in 1531 attacked Zurich. Zwingli died on the field of battle at Cappel, and was succeeded by Heinrich Bullinger.

M   Next to Luther, Calvin is the greatest man of the Reformation era. He was born in Noyon, France, of a well placed family, and as a young noble studied first for the priesthood in Paris and then as a law student in Orleans. Calvin was a brilliant student, and his Humanist studies of the classics coupled with his legal training made him eventually one of the greatest theologians in the history of the church.

In 1532, at the death of his father, Calvin joined a group of Protestants in Paris, but was forced to flee a year later because of his outspoken evangelical views. He was befriended by Martin Bucer, the great theological scholar at the University of Strasburg, and settled in Basel, where in 1536 he wrote his most famous work, THE INSTITUTES OF THE CHRISTIAN RELIGION. This is generally considered the clearest and most comprehensive statement of the Reformed faith ever written.

That same year Calvin was invited by the Protestant pastor of Geneva, William Farel, to stay in that city and help him combat the immorality that had come in under the guise of Christian liberty. Calvin immediately prepared articles of faith, a form of church government and a catechism for children. He advocated enforcing the existing laws against gambling, drunkeness, etc., and asked for permission to excommunicate unworthy church members. This was too much for the city government of Geneva, who expelled both Calvin and Farel.

N   For three years Calvin was pastor to French refugees in Strasburg, during which time he met Martin Luther and Phillip Malanchthon. Finally the responsible people in Geneva realized that only the measures that Calvin had proposed would save the city from anarchy. They implored him to return as pastor, and he reluctantly accepted after urging by his friends, realizing that this was the will of God.

Calvin lived and worked in Geneva for twenty four years until his death in O 1564. He preached and lectured several times a week, and sought to create in Geneva a model Christian community. Geneva became a haven for many great men of the Reformation, including John Knox and Theodore Beza, who followed Calvin. His ECCLESIASTICAL ORDINANCES set up a church governing board called a Consistory, made up of pastors and elders, which dealt with the spiritual matters of the community. Because most citizens of the city were baptized into the church as infants, spiritual principles derived from the Scriptures affected everyone (theoretically, at least). Consequently, the consistory was able to enforce morality by asking the civil authorities to impose penalties when necessary.

Calvin saw the doctrine of the sovereignty of God as the pivotal truth in theology, and put great stress on God's election as a necessary element in man's salvation. Thus he is often seen as the father of a very severe view of God who by His sovereign will chooses some and rejects others. Calvinists argue that this simplistic idea of the doctrine of election does not do justice to Calvin, and that one needs to read his works before drawing conclusions.

* * * * *

THE CHURCH OF ENGLAND

The fourth branch of the Reformation came into being in England and, as P the Church of England or the Anglican Church, is the official religious body there today. In the United States it is called the Episcopal Church, meaning that there is a line of spiritual authority extending from the parish priest or vicar up through a bishop of the diocease and finally to the Archbishop of Canterbury. In England the monarch is the secular head of the church.

The Reformation in England followed a different pattern than in Germany Q or Switzerland (but similar to Scandinavia) in that it had political beginnings from the top as well as a spiritual groundswell among the people. Henry VIII, king of England from 1509 until 1547, started his reign as a staunch Catholic. He wrote a treatise, ON THE SEVEN SACRAMENTS, in answer to Luther, which earned him the papal title Defender of the Faith. But Henry grew dissatisfied with his wife, Catherine of Aragon, who in the twenty-four years of their marriage had produced only one living child, a girl named Mary. Catherine was the widow of Henry's deceased brother, Arthur, and the marriage, arranged by Henry VII and Ferdinand of Spain, Catherine's father, had required a dispensation from the pope. By 1526 Henry had fallen in love with Anne Boleyn, a beautiful lady-in-waiting of the queen's court. With the help of Cardinal Wolsey, who was both the king's chancellor and the papal legate, he sought an annulment. The pope, in fear of the Emperor Charles V, Catherine's nephew, refused. The events that followed brought a permanent break with Rome and made England, politically, a Protestant nation.

R   Henry's motive for wanting the divorce was not simply one of passion for another woman, as the popular version of the story would have it. The bloody Wars of the Roses of the previous century were fought over the royal succession, and lack of a male heir could lead to more of the same and destroy England as a nation. Moreover, Henry quite likely had sincere doubts about God's will in the matter of his marriage to Catherine. In 1529 he deposed Wolsey and secured a divorce in one of his own courts. He also called together the so-called Reformation Parliament which passed the Act of Appeals providing that all English cases involving the clergy or church affairs be tried in England, forbade the payment of annates to the pope, and settled the throne on the heirs of Henry and Anne Boleyn. Later it abolished the monasteries. The Act of Supremacy of 1534 recognized the Anglican Church with Henry as its head. Henry married Anne Boleyn in January of 1533, she was crowned in the summer and gave birth to a daughter, Elizabeth, in September.

S   Henry made Thomas Cranmer, a devout and scholarly but somewhat weak willed man, the Archbishop of Canterbury in 1532. Two brilliant men, Bishop John Fisher and Sir Thomas More, he executed for opposing him. Henry was hardly a Reformer in any spiritual sense and toward the end of his life had laws passed, notably the Act of Six Articles, upholding celibacy of the clergy, transsubstantiation, prayers for the dead, etc. He imprisoned Godly preachers like Hugh Latimer, and a number of Christians suffered the death penalty for their Biblical beliefs. However, he also decreed that every church should have a copy of the Bible in English. The first English Bible translated from original languages by William Tyndale was now illegal in England and copies were being burned. Henry naturally rejected this version and accepted instead, in 1537, a version called Matthew's Bible which, ironically, was largely based on the Tyndale. William Tyndale, before his execution in 1536, had prayed that God would "open the king of England's eyes."

VII The Post-Reformation

THE LUTHERAN REFORMATION IN SCANDINAVIA

A   At the beginning of the 16th century all of Scandinavia was governed by Danish kings, and there was much nationalistic tension. The German Hanseatic League, a trading organization, exercized great power and added to the political ferment. In 1520 the Danish king, Christian II (1513-1523), for political reasons, introduced Lutheranism by securing a Lutheran preacher, Martin Reinhard. That same year, however, he massacred the leaders of the national Swedish party, whereupon Gustav Vasa organized a successful revolt and became King Gustavus I. Sweden then became the strongest Baltic power, holding back Russia, defeating Poland and sending armies to aid the Protestants in the

German wars of religion later in the century. Gustavus secularized church lands, a program of church reform was carried out, and most of the clergy came over to Lutheranism. The spiritual leader of the Swedish Reformation, however, was Olavus Petri (1493-1552), an associate of Luther. His literary work included Bible translations, a Swedish hymn book, devotional literature and historical works. His younger brother, Laurentius (1499-1573), became the first Lutheran archbishop of Sweden in 1531.

In Denmark, meanwhile, Christian II was driven from the throne and succeeded by his uncle, Frederick I (1523-33), who was sympathetic to reform. Hans Tausen (1494-1561), a former monk and Wittenburg student, through his powerful preaching became known as the "Danish Luther." A Danish New Testament was published in 1523. The next ruler, Christian III (1534-1558), secularized church land and established a Lutheran national church on a plan provided by Johann Bugenhagen, another friend of Luther. Bugenhagen consecrated seven new bishops and also reorganized the university.

Norway (which remained under the Danish crown until 1814) became Protestant at about the same time as Denmark, though with little popular support. The archbishop fled into exile, two bishops became Lutheran and the rest were expelled. Christian III also brought the Reformation to Iceland. Through the hymns and Bible translation of G. Thorlaksson, the Old Norse tongue was saved and the Reformation became popular. Finland became Lutheran through the efforts of Michael Agricola and Peter Sarkilax.

Toward the end of the 16th century the sons of Gustav Vasa attempted to get rid of the bishops and promote a Calvinistic church. Their successor, Sigismund, was a devout Catholic and endeavored to restore the old religion. He was deposed, but Sweden retained a peculiar mixture of old customs and Lutheranism.

EVENTS IN ENGLAND AFTER HENRY VIII

When Henry VIII died in 1547 (having been outlived by his sixth queen,   B
Catherine Parr), the country was in ferment. Much unrest had been caused by the dissolution of the monasteries and the turning out of thousands of monks and nuns, and also by the enclosure (or fencing) of public lands. Loyalties of the church were polarized toward the Protestants or toward Rome. The new king was Edward VI, son of Jane Seymour, Henry's third wife. He was ten years old. Edward had been given Christian training by Cranmer, and his brief reign swept away the repressive measures enacted by Henry. The first English prayer book was published in 1549, later replaced in 1552 by the Second Prayer Book which was definitely Protestant (and is still in use). Scholars like Ridley and Hooper, who had been in touch with the Reformers in Switzerland, returned to England. Where the bishops would not accept the reforming measures, they were replaced by Protestants. Martin Bucer came from Strasburg to become Professor of Theology at Cambridge. There was much pressure to reform or

"purify" the Church of England even more completely, on the model of Geneva. Hence the name "Puritan" came into being. True Reformation had come at last, but for many it had come too precipitously and at the cost of moderation. Again the pendulum was poised to swing.

C   Edward VI died on July 6, 1553, and was succeeded by Mary, daughter of Catherine of Aragon, a fanatical Romanist. During Edward's brief reign there was, unfortunately, considerable misgovernment on the part of the protectors, the Dukes of Somerset and Northumberland, and this aided Mary's cause. Northumberland sought to continue Protestant control of the country by crowning Lady Jane Grey, the 16 year old grandniece of Henry, but the plot failed and both Northumberland and the innocent Lady Jane died on the block at the Tower of London. Mary was determined to return England to the Catholic fold. All preaching and printing without her license was prohibited. Cranmer, Ridley, Coverdale, Hooper and Latimer were imprisoned and replaced by bishops loyal to Rome.

D   In 1554 Mary married her cousin Philip II, son of Charles V, a union which proved utterly unsuccessful. Members of Parliament were forced to petition Cardinal Pole, the new papal legate, to be received back into the Catholic church. Terrible persecution began, and great men like John Rogers (Tyndale's successor in the translation of the Old Testament), Bishop Hooper of Gloucester and Bishops Ridley and Latimer were burned at the stake. Archbishop Cranmer was condemned, recanted, then in a final burst of courage retracted and was also sent to the stake. Altogether, 286 people were executed for their faith, the majority at Smithfield just north of the walls of London, and many more died in prison, earning the queen the nickname of "Bloody Mary."

E   Queen Elizabeth I, daughter of Henry VIII and Anne Boleyn, came to the throne of England upon the miserable death of her half-sister Mary in 1558. She was welcomed and supported by all religious factions except the extreme papists because there was confidence that Elizabeth stood for moderation in religious matters. She caused the acts against heretics, used so cruelly by Mary, to be repealed and even made room for Puritans in the re-constituted church. However, she had no love for the doctrines of Geneva, even though some of the Calvinists were her staunch supporters. This was a political matter with Elizabeth. The Vatican, which never accepted Henry's divorce, looked upon her as illigitimate, and France and Spain supported her cousin, Mary Queen of Scots. Thus it was to her advantage to maintain a Protestant church in order to have the solid backing of the majority of her subjects.

Elizabeth loved the pomp and ceremony of the Roman church, on the other hand, and she favored the prayer book of 1549 over that of 1552 because the earlier version had less of the Protestant influence. She insisted on certain changes in proposed articles regarding the communion to bring them nearer to the Lutheran position. Even then, the famous Thirty Nine Articles of 1562 are remarkably Calvinistic. Wise counselors such as William Cecil pursuaded her to help the Protestants in France, Holland and Scotland. But she suppressed gatherings of Christians who came together to study the Scriptures, and removed from his position at Cambridge the great Puritan divine Thomas Cartwright. While Elizabeth controlled the church, she was opposed by Parliament, which was led by two strong Christian men, Strickland and Wentworth, who favored the Puritans. This clash between Crown and Parliament led eventually to civil war in the 17th century. Elizabeth's popularity suffered because of her imperious politics and the ruthless way she suppressed opposition, but it soared with the defeat of the Great Spanish Armada in 1588. Despite her faults, Elizabeth is regarded by historians as one of the greatest of English sovereigns and the one during whose reign England was united as a Protestant nation.

THE REFORMED CHURCH IN THE NETHERLANDS

The Netherlands (which included present day Belgium and Holland) were   F ruled by Charles V as part of the Holy Roman Empire when the Reformation began in Germany. The northern part (Holland) quickly accepted Luther's teachings and people began to study the Bible. Thus there was fertile ground for the reformed theology of Calvin a short time later. Belgium, on the other hand, remained Catholic, partly because Charles maintained his court at Flanders and exerted a heavy influence.

When Charles resigned, the empire was split between his brother Ferdinand, who got the eastern part, and his son Philip, who inherited the Netherlands (along with Spain, Milan, Naples, Sicily, etc.). Philip introduced the infamous Inquisition in Holland in 1555, and it became an offense to read the Bible. This reign of terror, during which many Christians were burned or beheaded, was met by organized resistance under William the Silent, prince of Orange. In 1572 the seven northern provinces formed the nucleus of the modern Dutch nation in the Utrecht Union.

In 1578 Amsterdam sided with the prince of Orange, and the Dutch Reformed Church became the official church. For a time dissention was suppressed, but during the 17th century there was a large amount of tolerance and Amsterdam became the gathering place for divergent religious groups including Jews from Portugal, Lutherans from Germany and Separatists from England. The English Reformed Church in Amsterdam (still being used) was founded in 1607, and the role of Holland in the saga of the Mayflower Pilgrims is well known.

THE REFORMED CHURCH IN FRANCE

The Reformation had come to France very early. By the mid-16th century   G there were a great many Christians who followed Calvin's doctrines. By 1558 these Protestants, or Huguenots as they were called, had some 2000 places of worship. But Francis I, son of Catherine de Medici, was committed to keeping the country Catholic. In the city of Provence, four thousand Waldenses were massacred by his army in 1545. Then, on the night of August 24, 1572, came the diobolical St. Bartholomew's Day Massacre, masterminded partly by the queen mother. 2000 Huguenots were murdered in Paris alone, and some 20,000 throughout France, including Admiral Coligny and other nobles. Not until 1598, through the Edict of Nantes, were the French Protestants granted religious freedom.

THE REFORMED CHURCH IN HUNGARY AND NORTHERN ITALY

H   Calvinism became the major form of Protestantism in Hungary, although Protestants there were persecuted for two centuries, gaining toleration finally in 1781. By the 19th century Hungary had the second largest Presbyterian church in the world. The Waldenses, who had suffered persecution since Medieval times, became a branch of the Reformed Church with a Presbyterian policy in 1532. However, they did not enjoy religious freedom until 1848.

THE REFORMED CHURCH IN SCOTLAND

I   In Scotland the Reformation took the form already developed in Geneva. The term Presbyterian stems from English speaking Reformers who associated with Calvin at Geneva, including John Knox. Thus the Scottish branch of the Reformed Church is called the Presbyterian Church. Presbytery is simply another word for Consistory, the governing board of the church.

Disgraceful conditions among the clergy in Scotland made the need for reform obvious by the 16th century, and Scotland had already come under the influence of John Hus, of the Lollards and of Luther. In 1528 a godly preacher, Patrick Hamilton, was burnt in front of St. Salvator College, St. Andrews, and this was followed by persecution of Protestants, which was strongly resisted. The country at this time was under the control of France due to royal marriages, and French troops were in Scotland. Thus the Protestants were supported by Henry VIII and later by Elizabeth. There was much violence, and a number of battles involving French, Scottish and English armies, and finally England took Edinburgh in 1560. The Treaty of Edinburgh ended French and Catholic control.

The great Scottish divine, John Knox, who was associated with Reformers both in Edwardian England and in Switzerland, helped to draw up a statement of Reformed doctrine and a confession of faith. Later, when Queen Mary Stuart returned to Scotland determined to reestablish Catholicism, Knox was ready for her. A famous battle of the wills ensued, but Knox never wavered. Ultimately the Queen of Scots was deposed in favor of her infant son, James VI. She was finally executed in England.

After the death of Knox, the champion of the Presbyterian system was Andrew Melville, principal of Glasgow University and later of St. Andrews. His work resulted in the recognition of the Church of Scotland by Parliament in 1592.

THE COUNTER-REFORMATION AND THE THIRTY YEARS WAR   1545-1648

J   The Counter-Reformation is a name given to a movement in the Catholic Church in the 16th century which included reaction to the Protestant Reformation. It was on the one hand a movement that corrected abuses such as the tendency for the clergy to be worldly and to neglect the spiritual needs of the people. Its new fervor of piety and dedication was seen in the founding of new orders like the Jesuits and the Capuchins, in missionary work like that of Francis Xavier, in mystical Christian writings like those of St. Teresa of Avila and St. John of the Cross, read by many evangelicals today.

On the other hand, the Counter-Reformation was a crusade to regain terri- K
tories lost to the Protestants, in the beginning by an attempt at reconciliation
and later by actual warfare. The new light from the study of the Scriptures was
spreading from North Germany, North Switzerland and Bohemia east to Austria
and Poland, south into Bavaria, Italy and Spain, and west to the northern Netherlands. In the end the Inquisition, a kind of religious secret police action, destroyed Protestantism in Italy and Spain. Austria was returned to the Catholic
fold by force under the Emperor Ferdinand II in the 17th century, Poland by
politics. The Catholic status of Bavaria and Bohemia and the Protestant status
of Holland and Switzerland were an outcome of the Thirty Years War.

The Council of Trent was called by Pope Paul III under pressure by the   L
Emperor Charles V who, seeing the Protestant revolt only in a political light,
hoped that the religious differences in Germany might be mended by compromise. The Council met at intervals from 1545 to 1563 and, being dominated by
forces loyal to the pope, succeeded only in clarifying the issues which divided
the two bodies in Christendom. In particular, there were the authority of the
pope, the authority of the teachings of the church as being equal with Scripture,
and the validity of the traditional sacraments and ceremonies of Catholicism.

The Thirty Years War began as a conflict between the Protestant and   M
Catholic elements in Germany, but ended as a full scale political struggle in
Europe involving the armies of a number of nations. It started in May, 1618,
when the Protestant Bohemians revolted against Ferdinand II, the Holy Roman
Emperor, and crowned Frederick V as king of Bohemia (Western Czechoslovakia). This tipped a balance of power in the Protestants' favor and brought
on a violent Catholic reaction. The Catholic forces were victorious in the Battle
of White Mountain, and by 1623 Frederick had been driven out of power. However, France under Cardinal Richelieu (Louis XIII's Minister of State), Sweden
under King Gustavus Adolphus and Denmark under Christian IV entered the war
on the Protestant side over fear that all of Europe would be dominated by
Imperial Germany. The war came to an end through the Peace of Westphalia
enacted at Munster in 1648. This established the religious lines of modern
European states and won a measure of tolerance for Protestants and Catholics
living in one another's territories. It proved that neither Catholic nor Protestant can totally liquidate the other where there is substantial support for both
sides, and therefore must find a way of co-existing. This lesson has yet to be
learned in some parts of the world today, though religious toleration is the rule
in most parts of Western Europe.

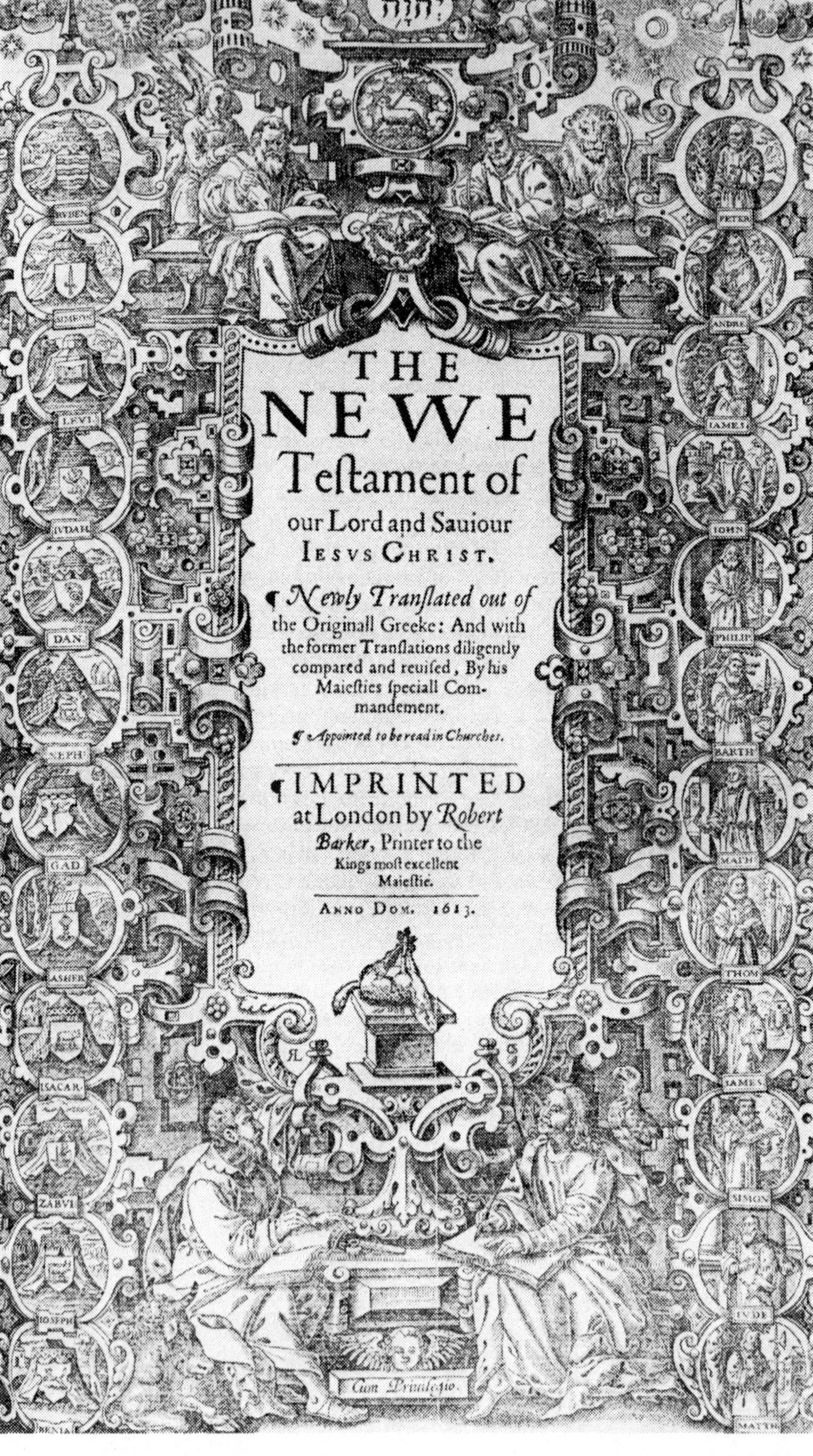
THE NEWE Testament of our Lord and Sauiour IESVS CHRIST.
Newly Translated out of the Originall Greeke: And with the former Translations diligently compared and reuised, By his Maiesties speciall Commandement.
¶ Appointed to be read in Churches.
¶ IMPRINTED at London by Robert Barker, Printer to the Kings most excellent Maiestie.
ANNO DOM. 1613.
Cum Priuilegio.

VIII The Seventeenth Century

The 17th century was a momentous period for the church in England, and   A
events occurred that permanently affected the course of Christianity in the
western world. The American colonies were founded, the King James version
of the Bible came into being, the Westminster Confession was drafted, the
Baptist, Congregational and Friends churches were established, John Milton
wrote PARADISE LOST and John Bunyan wrote THE PILGRIM'S PROGRESS.
On the other hand, it was one of the most troubled periods in English history
and the first (and only) instance in which the English people put their sovereign
to death. The scars of the terrible distructiveness of the Civil War can still
be seen in castles, cathedrals and great houses throughout England.

JAMES I AND THE PURITANS
James VI of the Scottish House of Stuart became James I of England in 1603 B
upon the death of Elizabeth, his mother's cousin. Thus ended the famous Tudor
dynasty. James was no more tolerant of the Puritans than his predecessor, and
was committed to the concept of the "divine right of kings" and to the Episco-
palian system. The Puritans stood for simplicity in worship and in the authority
of Scripture, as do a great many evangelicals today. Vicious and ignorant
propaganda has painted them as joyless drabs, but this was true only in extreme
cases. They numbered among them great artists such as Edmund Spencer,
Sir Philip Sydney, John Milton and Andrew Marvel, and a great many scholars.
James called church leaders together at a conference at Hampton Court in
1604, during which he publicly insulted the Puritans. However, he did accept
the suggestion of Dr. Reynolds of Oxford, a Puritan, that a new version of the
Bible was needed, and out of this the so-called King James version of 1611 came
into being. Later, James demanded by royal proclamation complete conformity
to the order of worship of the Church of England and persecuted those who refused to sign the new canons. Many ministers were ousted and some imprisoned.
A new archbishop, Abbot, influenced James to authorize the Irish Articles in
1615, giving the Puritans freedom there. Under Bishop Ussher (the chronologer)
Ireland became a place of refuge for evangelicals from England and Scotland.

THE PILGRIM FATHERS

C   In the year 1620, during the reign of King James I, a group of Christians who were called Separatists, but whom we now call the Pilgrim Fathers, sailed from Plymouth to found a colony in Massachusetts. This group came originally from the village of Scrooby in Nottinghamshire. Like many nonconformist churches today, they rejected the principle of a national church. Their pastor, John Robinson, developed the concept of local church government, later called "Congregationalism." The idea spread and some pastors who practiced it were put to death. In 1608, led by Robinson and William Brewster, the group moved to Holland but were unhappy there, primarily because their children began to identify with the Dutch culture. They returned to England in 1620 and sailed for the New World that same year, arriving in December. Despite extreme hardships the colony flourished, and by 1640 twenty thousand had immigrated to New England.

THE BAPTISTS

D   In 1611 a group which had separated from an English congregation in Amsterdam over the issue of infant baptism came to London under the leadership of Thomas Helwys. Helwys had the impropriety to publish a book in which he penned a special inscription on the fly leaf of a presentation copy to King James which read, "The king is a mortall man and not God, therefore hath not power over the immortal soules of his subjects . . ." He was thrown into Newgate Prison and never heard from again. The body of Christians led by Helwys were called Baptists because they maintained that only adults professing faith in Christ should be baptized, and children not at all. The group grew and multiplied until there were Baptist churches throughout Britain and Europe. The most famous Baptist of the 17th century was John Bunyan, a tinker of Bedford, who wrote his immortal allegory, PILGRIM'S PROGRESS, during a prison term for illegal preaching. Bunyan is buried in the nonconformist cemetery in London.

UNITARIANISM AND ARMINIANISM

E   Two 17th century theologians who still have an impact upon Christianity today are Faustus Socinus and Jacobus Arminius. Socinus, an Italian, was the founder of Unitarianism, which follows the Congregational form of church government but rejects the essential Christian doctrines. Unitarianism became very popular in England and later New England. Arminius, a professor at Leyden, Holland, objected to the Calvinist teaching of predestination. According to his view, Christ made atonement for all men, but only believers benefit. It is possible to resist the work of the Holy Spirit, and it is possible for believers to lapse from the faith and be lost. Arminianism became the official view of the Methodists in the 18th century, and was accepted by some Congregationalists and Baptists. It is the position of Pentecostal and Holiness groups today.

CHARLES I AND CIVIL WAR

James was followed by Charles I, who continued similar policies to his   F
father in government and church. He was supported by the notorious Archbishop
Laud. Pressure against the Puritans, who dominated Parliament, was stepped up.
Laud began to again refer to the communion table as the "altar" and to bow to it.
In 1629 the House of Commons revolted and was adjourned for eleven years, while
while Charles reigned as a despot. Puritans were subjected everywhere to fines,
imprisonment and torture. In 1640 the famous Long Parliament convened, and
refused to vote any money until religious grievances were redressed. The "Root
and Branch Petition", signed by fifteen thousand Londoners, demanded that the
episcopal church government be abolished. Parliament sent to the king the Grand
Remonstrance which set forth his many acts of misgovernment, and Charles's
attempt to arrest the instigators failed. Civil war began in August, 1642.

Early in the war the Parliamentarians lost some of their top leadership, and G
the Royalists had the upper hand. Eventually the former appealed to the Scots for
help. In Scotland, no General Assemblies had been permitted, and the King and
Laud had tried to force the Church of England liturgy and the new canons on the
Presbyterian ministers. On February 28, 1638, the National Covenant had been
signed in Greyfriars Church, Edinburgh, binding its signatories by an oath to
maintain the freedom of the Presbyterian Church, and copies were signed all
over the land. The General Assembly met in November of that year, the first
time since 1596 and, led by the Moderator Alexander Henderson, abolished the
Church of England canons and formally established Presbyterianism. Thus the
Scots were ready to respond to the call to fight for their faith.

In 1643 the Scots and the English Parliamentarians entered into the Solemn   H
League and Covenant, binding themselves to seek the reformation of religion
according to the Reformed pattern of Geneva. The Westminster Assembly of
Divines met from 1643 to 1649 with the object of finding a basis for a united
church for the whole of Britain. The result was the Westminster Confession,
adopted in Scotland in 1647, and the backbone of Presbyterian churches throughout the world today.

The Scots army under the brilliant generals Alexander and David Leslie   I
were successful against the Royal forces in the north. Many bloody battles
were fought during the years between 1642 and 1646. The Parliamentarian
general, Oliver Cromwell, ultimately gained the upper hand, and in the end
achieved crushing victories. England paid a bitter price as the soldiers of both
sides ravaged the countryside, looting, vandalizing and sometimes completely
destroying many of the most beautiful buildings in the land. In the English
Parliament, a military junta prevailed, and Charles I was condemned to death
and beheaded outside Whitehall Banqueting House, London, on January 30, 1649.

OLIVER CROMWELL

J   Oliver Cromwell ruled England as a kind of military dictator from 1649 until his death in 1658. He was a devout and sincere Christian, concerned about doing the will of God according to the Scriptures, but he took upon himself the responsibility of trying to make a Christian theocracy work in an imperfect society, a task too great for any mere man. The period of the Commonwealth is generally considered one of England's most inglorious epochs. One bright light was Cromwell's Latin secretary, John Milton, whose Christian epics PARADISE LOST and PARADISE REGAINED stand among the world's literary classics. Perhaps Cromwell's most positive contribution to the cause of the Christian faith was to make Parliament and not the king the final authority on ecclesiastical questions in the Church of England.

IRELAND UNDER CROMWELL

K   In 1649-50 Cromwell moved to subjugate Ireland. His troops took the Irish stronghold·of Drogheda and liquidated several thousand people, an act for which history has condemned him severely. He succeeded in his goal of transfering the land from Irish to British proprietors, but failed to make Ireland Protestant.

CHRISTIAN POETS OF THE 17TH CENTURY

L   During the great conflict between Puritans and Anglicans during the 17th century, literature naturally tended to reflect this life and death struggle, and the writers' sense of the complexities and contradictions of life. Among the poets of this period were several devout and sincere Christians, including the dean of St. Paul's Cathedral, John Donne (acknowledged leader of the "Metaphysical School" of poets), George Herbert, Richard Crashaw, Henry Vaughan, Thomas Traherne, and the beloved author of THE COMPLEAT ANGLER Isaak Walton.

CHARLES II AND THE RESTORATION

M   Charles II, the executed monarch's son, as early as 1650 returned from the Continent to Scotland in an effort to rally followers behind restoring the monarchy. The Scots, alienated by Cromwell's government, supported him, though some prominent men like the great scholar of divinity Samuel Rutherford were opposed. Charles was crowned first at Scone, where he swore hypocritically to support the Solemn League and Covenant. Then, in 1660, Parliament invited him to accept the throne of England. By the Declaration of Breda, Charles promised leniency to those who had participated in the rebellion, and to grant religious liberty. However, Parliament, now dominated by the Royalists, proved to be strongly Anglican. Four acts were passed which were directed particularly against the Independents or nonconformists. These renounced the Solemn League and Covenant and made it practically impossible for any church to legally exist but the Church of England.

JOHN BUNYAN AND GEORGE FOX

Two famous Englishmen who refused to obey the new acts were the Baptist N
John Bunyan, already mentioned, and George Fox. Fox founded the Society of
Friends, nicknamed the Quakers, and he and many of the Friends suffered
severely. A large number emigrated to North America, among them the young
aristocrat William Penn. The colony of Pennsylvania, which he founded in 1682,
became a model for religious tolerance in an age when this concept was
virtually unknown.

THE COVENANTERS

In Scotland, the Presbyterian Covenanters soon found that they had wel-　O
comed a wolf into the fold. Charles soon attempted to impose Episcopacy upon
the Scottish church. The Covenanters resisted with arms and were disastrously
defeated. They then organized the Presbyterian Societies which met secretly in
the mountains and moorlands. They were hunted down by the king's men, and
over 17,000 suffered in one way or another. Hundreds were executed at the
Mercat Cross and in the Grass Market of Edinburgh.

THE GREAT LONDON PLAGUE AND FIRE

In the winter of 1665-66 there occurred in London a hideous plague which　P
took the lives of some 70,000 people. This was followed, in the latter part of
1666, by the great fire of London which destroyed a good part of the old city
including old St. Paul's Cathedral. In the wake of these calamaties, the king's
chief minister, Clarendon, who was responsible for the various acts of
religious intolerance, was banished.

Toward the end of his life Charles was enabled to live independently from
Parliamentary grants because of money received from France's Louis XIV.
Part of a secret deal which Charles had made was that he would turn Catholic
in time, but he found it expedient to drop this plan and work with the Anglicans.

THE HUGUENOTS

Louis XIV, the despotic "Sun King" of France, found it advantageous to　Q
support the French Catholics in 1682 so that they might enjoy the "Gallican
Liberties" and be free from the intervention of the pope in the temporal
affairs of the nation. However, the Protestants did not fare so well. In 1685 his
policy led to the revocation of the Edict of Nantes (1598) that had given
Protestants religious freedom. Some 400,000 Huguenots fled to other countries,
including Britain and America.

JAMES II AND THE GLORIOUS REVOLUTION

R   The last of the Stuart kings was James II, the brother of Charles II and an avowed Catholic. Rebellion arose in Scotland during his reign headed by Argyle, chief of the Campbell clan, but it was crushed by the royal army. The exiled Duke of Monmouth, Charles's illegitimate son and a Protestant, returned to England and also raised a rebellion. He, too, suffered defeat and death. The "Bloody Assizes" presided over by the infamous Judge Jeffries condemned more than three hundred of Monmouth's followers to death as well. Richard Baxter, famous Presbyterian divine and the author of many books, was one of those later sent to prison by Jeffries. In 1688 the Glorious Revolution occurred when the Opposition called to England William of Orange, king of Holland, and Mary his wife, the daughter of James II. James fled to France in order to save his skin.

        The reign of William and Mary brought peace and stability on both civil and religious levels. In England, the Anglican Church became the approved religious body, and in Scotland the Presbyterian Church and the Westminster Confession were established under the Revolution Settlement of 1689-90. The Toleration Act of 1689 improved the position of the nonconformists. Three parties became distinguishable within the Church of England - - High, Evangelical and Broad - - and this distinction is still true to some extent today.

IX The Eighteenth Century

A   The 18th century, sometimes called The Age Of Reason, was a period in which the various bodies of Christians in Europe no longer had to defend their faith in the face of fire or sword. The new method of inductive investigation in science and the refinement of society led people to believe that all the problems of the universe could be solved by the rational mind of man. Applied to Christianity, this led to Deism, the belief that God is remote and that the universe is ruled by natural (and discoverable) laws. Deism gave rise to Unitarianism (already established since the 17th century) among the Presbyterians and Baptists, and Latitudinarianism among the Anglicans. From England, Deism spread to Germany where it was called "The Enlightenment." In France, it influenced a group of brilliant scholars called the Encyclopaedists. Eventually these ideas developed into the philosophy of Rationalism.

THE PIETISTS

B   In Germany, a very important evangelical group from about 1670 were the Pietists, who were highly influenced by the writings of John Bunyan and Richard Baxter. Their views were similar to the English Puritans. The wealthy Count Zinzendorf was a Pietist convert, and allowed a group of Moravian Brethren (followers of John Hus) to settle on his lands. The Moravians became pioneers of the modern foreign missionary movement.

THE EVANGELICAL REVIVAL

The dead orthodoxy of the established churches in 18th century Britain was   C
sharply contrasted by revivals which swept the land during the same period.
These are primarily associated with the names of George Whitefield and John
Wesley, though a number of other men of God were involved. The revivals
occurred mainly among the miners and other working classes, but they affected
people on every level of society.

John Wesley was an Oxford student when he organized the "Holy Club,"   D
together with his brother Charles. This put a great emphasis on regular spiritual
exercize, and thus its members came to be called "Methodists" because they were
were methodical in their devotions. In 1736 John Wesley went to Georgia as a
missionary and failed miserably. However, on the voyage out and also in Georgia
he had contact with the Moravian Brethren, who influenced him profoundly. On
May 24, 1738, at a meeting of an evangelical society in Aldersgate Street, London,
Wesley (as he wrote in his journal) ". . . felt I did trust in Christ, Christ alone,
for salvation."

Wesley soon launched into one of the most remarkable evangelistic minis-   E
tries that the world has ever known. For fifty years he criss-crossed England
on horseback, generally following a triangle made up of London, Bristol and
Newcastle-Upon-Tyne, traveling some 250,000 miles to preach to untold thousands, mostly in the open air. His brother Charles, converted at about the same
time, was his helper and calm companion. The hymns of Charles Wesley - -
for example, "And Can It Be That I Should Gain An Interest In the Savior's
Blood" and "O For A Thousand Tongues To Sing My Great Redeemer's Praise"
- - are found in the majority of Christian hymnbooks today. Through the efforts
of the Wesley brothers and others who followed after them such as Thomas Coke
and Francis Asbury the Methodist Church came into being.

George Whitefield, who shares equal honors with John Wesley as a leader   F
of the evangelical revival of the 18th century, was also a member of the "Holy
Club" at Oxford. Whitefield at first associated with Wesley in evangelistic work,
but disagreed with him on the matter of the availability of salvation. While
Wesley took the Arminian view, Whitefield adopted Calvinism. He made an early
visit to Georgia in response to an invitation by John Wesley, remaining there
from 1737 to 1741. In England, he followed much the same pattern of open air
preaching as the Wesleys, but also made longer journeys including no less than
seven trips to America. He was one of the most eloquent preachers in the history
of the English church, but unlike Wesley did not found a church of his own. The
poet William Cowper wrote of him:

> "He followed Paul - - his zeal a kindred flame,
> His apostolic charity the same."

CHARLES SIMEON

G   Another important 18th century evangelical was Charles Simeon, who became vicar of Holy Trinity Church, Cambridge, in 1782 at the age of 23. His saintly life and Biblical preaching made a profound impression among the students, a number of whom dedicated their lives to the evangelization of the heathen in foreign lands. Henry Martyn, for whom a hall in the church is now named, spent his short life in translation work in India and Persia. Simeon is generally felt to be the father of the Cambridge Inter-Collegiate Christian Union which came into being officially in the 1870's. The C. I. C. C. U., in turn, became the inspiration for a national and later an international movement of evangelical students.

18TH CENTURY HYMNWRITERS

H   The 18th century produced a number of great hymnwriters besides Charles Wesley. Among these are Isaac Watts ("Jesus Shall Reign Where 'Ere the Sun"), John Newton ("How Sweet the Name Of Jesus Sounds"), William Cowper ("God Works In Mysterious Ways"), Augustus Toplady ("Rock Of Ages") and Philip Doddridge ("O Happy Day That Fixed My Choice").

SCOTLAND IN THE 18TH CENTURY

I   In 18th century Scotland, the Presbyterian Church settled into the same kind of dead orthodoxy as the Church of England. Splinter groups of evangelicals were started by Ebenezer Erskine, Thomas Gillespie and others, which eventually became the United Presbyterian Church. In 1740 a great revival began in Glasgow under William MacCulloch of the Church of Scotland. A young minister influenced by this, Dr. John Erskine (later of Greyfriars Church, Edinburgh), was for 60 years the leader of the evangelicals within the Church of Scotland. On the political side, there were three uprisings in the Scottish Highlands (1715, 1719, 1745) aimed at bringing back the "Old Pretender" (James, son of James II) and the "Young Pretender" (Charles, grandson of James II, also known as "Bonnie Prince Charlie"). These were crushed by the English redcoats, thus assuring that the British monarchy must remain Protestant.

THE FRENCH REVOLUTION

J   Besides being the Age of Reason, the 18th century was also the Age of Revolutions. The American Revolution of the 1770's produced a new state with religious freedom guaranteed by a written constitition. The French Revolution (1789-1794), on the other hand, occurred partly because of the abuses perpetrated by the Roman Catholic Church. Thus, in a sense the French Revolution was a revolt against a corrupt form of Christianity. The king, Louis XVI, his queen, Marie Antoinette, and thousands of nobles and "suspects" were sent to the guillotine in the infamous Reign of Terror. Napoleon Bonaparte then gained power and, in 1796, occupied Rome with his armies. The Pope was forced to cede one third of his territories. Later, in 1801, Napoleon entered into a "Concordat" with the papacy under which all bishops had to resign and new ones were nominated by Napoleon.

X Beginnings of Modern Missions

The establishment of European and British colonies in North America,   A
Africa and the Far East paved the way for the modern Protestant missionary
movement. In 1649 Parliament in England formed "the Corporation For the
Propagation of the Gospel in New England," with which John Eliot and the
Mayhew family are associated. Later, David Brainerd helped to arouse the
church to the mission field among North American Indians. Dutch missionaries,
influenced by Pietism, evangelized in the new colonies in Malaya, India and
Ceylon. August Herman Franke, a German Pietist at Halle University, in co-
operation with the king of Denmark's chaplain, organized the Danish-Halle
Mission to India in 1705. Ironically, the main opposition to this early missionary
work was from the trading companies of Britain, Holland and Denmark.

WILLIAM CAREY AND THE MISSIONARY SOCIETIES

One of the greatest of the pioneer missionaries was William Carey (1761-   B
1834), a former cobbler and Baptist minister. He helped to found the Baptist
Missionary Society in 1792 which led to a great movement of evangelism in
India. This was followed by the London Missionary Society, which was formed
in 1795 and the General Methodist Society in 1796. These were the direct result
of the great evangelical awaking in England during the 18th century.

THE CLAPHAM SECT

A group of wealthy and influential Christians who met for prayer and Bible   C
study at Clapham (on the southern outskirts of London) in the 1790's had a direct
influence upon the move led by William Wilberforce to abolish the slave trade.
The writer Hannah More, also associated with this group, helped to bring into
being the Religious Tract Society. The "Clapham Sect," through Charles Grant,
a wealthy East India merchant, had an important part in the founding of the
British and Foreign Bible Society. The Church Missionary Society, now the
largest missionary group in the British Commonwealth, was also an outgrowth
of the "Clapham Sect." Henry Martyn was one of their pioneer members.

XI The Nineteenth Century

A   The 19th century began at a time when vast social, economic and scientific changes were occurring in Britain and Europe. It was the age of transition between two worlds - - that of the 18th century characterized by hand, horse and wind power, and that of the 20th century utilizing electricity, the internal combustion engine and electronics. The concentration of the population in cities, the development of swift transportation, the influence of science on philosophy and religion, all had far reaching effects on the Christian church.

THE INDUSTRIAL REVOLUTION

B   The Industrial Revolution brought many social ills, and the church in Great Britain moved to try and correct them. Both the Anglicans and the nonconformists established school societies. Great Christian statesmen such as Lord Shaftsbury agitated to stop abuses in the factories.   Christina Rosetti and other writers raised an outcry over child labor. In 1783 Robert Raikes founded Sunday Schools with the object of teaching children to read the Bible. George Muller and Thomas Barnardo founded orphans' homes. In 1865 William Booth and his wife started the Salvation Army, designed to reach the thousands who lived in London's slums. Thus did the Christian church respond to the needs of humanity which emerging science and industry overlooked.

THE CHRISTIAN BRETHREN

C   The second largest nonconformist body (next to the Baptists) in Britain and Europe are the Christian Brethren, known popularly as the "Plymouth Brethren." This movement began in Dublin, Ireland, in 1827, and a former Anglican clergyman, John Nelson Darby, emerged as its strongest leader. The Brethren held that the position of the clergy in the established church is unscriptural and that all believers are priests, according to the New Testament. They also objected to the formalism of the church, especially the communion. Their assemblies stressed the development of gifts of teaching, etc., among all eligible Christians, the centrality of the Lord's Supper, the preaching of the Gospel, the study of the Bible and a system of Biblical interpretation stressing prophecy, called Dispensationalism.

    The first large assembly met at Plymouth, England, with Darby and B. W. Newton as leaders. Ultimately, Newton and Darby disagreed over prophecy and the Lord's Supper (Darby espousing a closed communion), and the movement split. Newton's followers joined a group in Bristol, one of whose leaders was the famed George Muller. Thus began the "Open Brethren." The Brethren movement (they prefer a small "b") spread to French speaking Switzerland and other parts of Europe, the British Empire and the United States. Brethren assemblies (who call their buildings Gospel halls, or more latterly, chapels or evangelical churches) are to be found today in every community in Britain and throughout Europe. In some countries such as Italy and Spain they constitute the major evangelical group.

THE OXFORD MOVEMENT

Another 19th century Christian movement in Britain destined to have con-   D
siderable influence on the church arose in Oxford under the leadership of John
Henry Newman, vicar of St. Mary's Church. A number of able men along with
Newman attempted to strengthen the position of the established church by
claiming unbroken continuity with the ancient Catholics. They propagated their
views through tracts, thus gaining the name "Tractarians," and the trend that
they started was called The Oxford Movement. Many Roman Catholic doctrines
such as apostolic succession and transubstantiation were revived in the Anglican
church as a result of the Oxford Movement, and there was a general glorification
of Medieval Christianity. Eventually, Newman became a Roman Catholic
cardinal and many of the other Tractarians joined the Roman church. Newman's
contribution to 19th century religious literature is considerable, and his hymn,
"Lead Kindly Light" is still well known.

OTHER 19TH CENTURY INFLUENCES ON THE CHURCH

The 19th century saw other forces come into being whose effects on the   E
church have been devastating. Such names as Karl Marx in political science,
John Stuart Mill and Herbert Spencer in philosophy and Charles Darwin in
natural science are all associated with Victorian England, in one sense the most
Christian nation on earth. From Germany during this period came the Graf-
Wellhausen theory of Biblical criticism which, as "higher criticism," is still
accepted in many theological circles.

Evangelism and missions also took a great leap forward in 19th century
England. Hudson Taylor founded the China Inland Mission in the 1860's. In 1882
D. L. Moody was invited by the Cambridge Inter-Collegiate Christian Union to
conduct a campaign at this university. A large number of students were con-
verted. Two years later seven brilliant young men, known as the "Cambridge
Seven," volunteered for overseas missionary service. These included C.T.
Studd, a champion cricketer, who became the founder of the Worldwide
Evangelization Crusade. Meanwhile, a student at Princeton University in
America, Robert Wilder, formed a group to pray that God would provide a
thousand missionary volunteers. In 1886, at a meeting presided over by D. L.
Moody, a hundred students volunteered and the Student Volunteer Movement
was launched. In a few years over nine thousand young people responded to the
rallying cry of "The evangelization of the world in this generation!".

XII The Twentieth Century

A   The 20th century dawned on an optimistic society in Britain and Europe.
Science was promising great things, and the long span of peace led people to
believe that the human race was evolving toward a bright future. D. L. Moody,
Charles Spurgeon and other great evangelical leaders were dead, and the
Christian church was strongly tainted by liberalism in doctrinal matters. It was
fashionable to send theology students to study in Germany, from which the most
radical theories of Biblical criticism emanated. Then came August, 1914, and
the optimism vanished in the smoke of battle. With World War I the gracious and
romantic age of Victoria ended in the horror of modern warfare, in which over
ten million young men were slain in the battlefields and trenches of Central
Europe. World War I ended on November 11, 1918.

BETWEEN THE WARS

B   The 20's and 30's turned out to be merely a pause between wars involving
most of Europe (and a good part of the rest of the world as well). During this
brief twenty year period a Christian view of Scripture known as Neo-Orthodoxy
or Neo-Calvinism was developed by a Swiss theologian, Karl Barth. This has
had far reaching effects upon the church throughout the western world. Some
years earlier, during World War I, Switzerland had also been host to a Bolshevik
revolutionary named Vladimir Lenin. In 1917 Lenin was transported into Russia,
and led the revolution which resulted in the Union of Soviet Socialist Republics.
The effect of the U. S. S. R. upon Christianity in Eastern Europe and throughout
the world is one of the most important aspects of church history in the 20th
century. When Lenin died in 1924 he was succeeded by Josef Stalin, who defeated
his political opponent Leon Trotsky in 1926 and 27.

C   Meanwhile, in Germany, a political radical named Adolph Hitler was jailed
in 1923 for attempting to overthrow the Bavarian government with his new
National Socialist Party. While in prison Hitler recorded his political and philo-
sophical theories in MEIN KAMPF. Ten years later, in 1933, Hitler and his
Nazis gained control of all Germany and launched one of the most complete over-
turns of society in European history. Predominent in their policy was the sup-
pression and ultimate liquidation of the Jews.

D   The story of the Christian church in Germany during the Hitler era is a
complex one. By and large the free churches (Baptists and brethren) remained
silent. The official state church, which became servile to Hitler, was opposed
before the war by a Confessing Church movement led by such men as Martin
Niemoller, Karl Barth (who, though Swiss, identified himself with the German
church), Hans Asmussen and Dietrich Bonhoeffer. After the war started in 1939
the Confessing Church virtually disappeared. Bonhoeffer, whose books such as
THE COST OF DISCIPLESHIP and LETTERS FROM PRISON are widely read
by evangelicals today, was arrested for his part in a plot to overthrow Hitler.

He was executed just before the end of the war. By VE Day in May, 1945, some six million Jews and other innocent victims had perished in the Nazi death camps scattered throughout Europe.

WORLD WAR II

In September, 1939, Poland was invaded by German forces, and in April and   E
May of 1940 Denmark, Norway, the Netherlands, Belgium and Luxembourg were overrun by the Germans. With the fall of France, the Battle of Britain began in June, 1940. Thousands died in the bombings, between 300 and 600 a day in London alone, and many priceless landmarks were destroyed, among them Coventry Cathedral which was leveled on November 10. As the tide of the war turned, the cities of Germany and Europe were likewise devastated by Allied air raids, the most striking example being the destruction of Dresden.

Christian pastors and chaplains, British Army Scripture Readers and other   F
servants of God played a vital role during and after the war. In London, an Anglican vicar named J.B. Phillips laboring among the bombing victims conceived the idea of putting the New Testament into a vernacular that his parishioners could understand with ease. The result was LETTERS TO YOUNG CHURCHES, first published in 1947, and followed in 1958 by THE NEW TESTAMENT IN MODERN ENGLISH. Meanwhile, an Oxford don and classical scholar, C.S. Lewis, read over the B.B.C. three series of Broadcast Talks, later amalgamated into a single volume, MERE CHRISTIANITY, perhaps the most influential apologetic of the Christian faith in the world today.

In Germany, two godly women, now known as Mother Basilea Schlink and   G
Mother Martyria, held Bible studies in an attic in Darmstadt while the bombing raged around them. Following the war, they founded the Evangelical Sisterhood of Mary and established a conference grounds called "Canaan" in 1948 as a witness to Jesus Christ. Many find spiritual nourishment in this non-denominational retreat each year. At the same time, a young British army officer, Major Ian Thomas, saw the need for bringing the Gospel to the vast numbers of "Hitler Youth." The outcome of this idea was the Bible training center, Capernwray Hall, in England and some eight Bible schools and conference centers throughout Europe which today play a significant role in reaching young people of the state churches. Meanwhile in Holland, a Christian family named ten Boom were arrested by the Nazis for sheltering Jews in their Haarlem home. Several of this family and their friends died in prison or concentration camps but one, Corrie, was miraculously released, and has spent the last 30 years telling people that "Jesus can turn loss into glory."

CHRISTIANITY IN EUROPE SINCE WORLD WAR II

During the more than 30 years since the end of World War II Europe has   H
undergone vast social, economic and religious changes. East Germany, Poland Czechoslovakia, Hungary, Romania, Bulgaria and Albania are satellite states to the U.S.S.R. as a result of agreements made by Stalin with Winston Churchill

and Franklin Roosevelt. Christians in these areas as well as in Russia itself have kept the faith through severe difficulties and outright persecution. The Scandinavian and Central European nations have prospered, Germany in particular, and with a rise in the standard of living has come a secularization that considers the church irrelevant. In these same countries the void left by the loss of interest in Christianity has been filled partly by materialism, partly by various forms of the occult and new religions. The low standards of public morals in Denmark, Sweden and even Holland with regard to pornography have shocked decent people everywhere.

On the other hand, an impressive amount of Biblical Christianity has arisen in Europe since 1945, partly through missions organizations from America and Britain, partly through Spirit filled pastors and national para-church evangelistic movements. International Congresses for World Evangelization have been held in the 1970's in Berlin and Lausanne, and Mission 76, a missionary convention for European young people, was held at Lausanne at the end of 1975. These and other all-Europe conferences held recently such as Spree 73 and Eurofest in 1975 indicate that the history of Christianity in Europe is by no means ended. It also means, however, that Europe is increasingly becoming alienated from its Christian past and needs to be considered a mission field much as the Irish monks found it in the 6th century.

The British Isles

Italy

Germany

Switzerland

The Netherlands

Belgium

France

Spain

Austria

Greece

Scandinavia

Eastern Europe

Portugal

SECTION B

THE
CHRISTIAN SIGHTS
IN EUROPE

The British Isles

Of all the places in the world where Christianity was carried in the first three centuries after Christ, nowhere did it take root more firmly nor flourish more productively than in the British Isles. In parts of Britain (Wales, for example) the church has continued in unbroken succession down to the present time. From these islands in the early centuries the rest of Europe was evangelized, and from the 18th century onward Britain has been a prime contributor to modern world missions. The majority of the church movements of the western world sprang from British origins, and Christianity remains (despite the social decay of the present times) the official religion of Britain and the Bible the official book.

With such a wealth of Christian backgrounds in one tiny area, it is logical therefore to begin our guide to Christian landmarks in Western Europe with the British Isles.

LONDON AND ENVIRONS

1. The Tower of London is London's top historical monument, and figures   VI-S
prominently in Christian history. First constructed in 1078 by William the   VII-C
Conqueror as a fortress, the Tower later became a political prison. During the
16th century, Sir Thomas More, Bishop John Fisher and a host of other Christians
both well known and obscure were detained here, as well as royal personages
such as Anne Boelyn and Lady Jane Grey. The Tower is so extensive that you
should allow at least a half day to do it justice. One dramatic way to approach
it (and the way many prisoners approached it) is by water down the Thames.
Get a public launch at the embankment near Westminster Bridge. Another
unusual way to experience the Tower is to view the celebrated "changing of the
keys" at 9-10:00 P. M. Apply for free tickets in writing (specifying what date you
want and how many tickets up to four or five) to the Governor of the Tower,
Tower of London. See also

The site of the scaffold near Tower Hill where the public executions took place (only a few of the royalty and nobility were executed privately inside the Tower). There are memorials to a number of famous victims.

All Hallows By the Tower Church. William Penn was baptized here on   VIII-N
October 23, 1644, and John Quincy Adams was married in this church.

III-G   2. Westminster Abbey, the royal church near the Houses of Parliament,
VI-Q   was started during the reign of Edward the Confessor, king of England before
V-B   the Norman invasion of 1066. Edward, and most of Britain's monarchs (up to
IX-D, E the 18th century) including Henry VIII and Elizabeth I are entombed here. The
coronation chair of England and the coronation stone of Scotland (Stone of Scone)
are in Edward the Confessor's Chapel, and all coronations from that of William
the Conqueror onward have taken place in this abbey. All royal weddings are
also performed here. On the main aisle in the nave is the grave of the great
missionary David Livingstone, over which is a brass plate with a stirring
memorial. The grave of Britain's unknown warrior is near the west entrance.
In Poet's Corner (south transept) are the graves of Chaucer, Browning,
Tennyson and others of Britain's chief literary figures (there are memorials to
many not actually buried here, also). Memorials to John and Charles Wesley
and to Isaac Watts are in the south aisle. A stained glass window in the north
transept honors John Bunyan.

     Westminster Abbey bookstore is near the main entrance, which has
books and other items related to the English church not often seen else-
where.

III-B   3. The British Museum is one of the greatest treasure houses of Christian
III-C   history in the world. The manuscript room contains such priceless items as
IV-C   the Codex Sinaiticus (oldest complete Bible in existence), the Gospel of
VI-Q   Thomas, the Lindisfarne Gospels, a Wycliffe Bible and manuscript letters of
Henry VIII, Anne Boleyn and other notable figures of the English Reformation.
The Near Eastern and Egyptian Antiquities collections are even more extensive,
including: the world famous Rosetta Stone (BM 24)
     a relief portrait of Sargon II, conqueror of Samaria (BM 118822)
     an obelisk depicting Jehu of Israel bowing before the king of
Assyria (BM 118885)

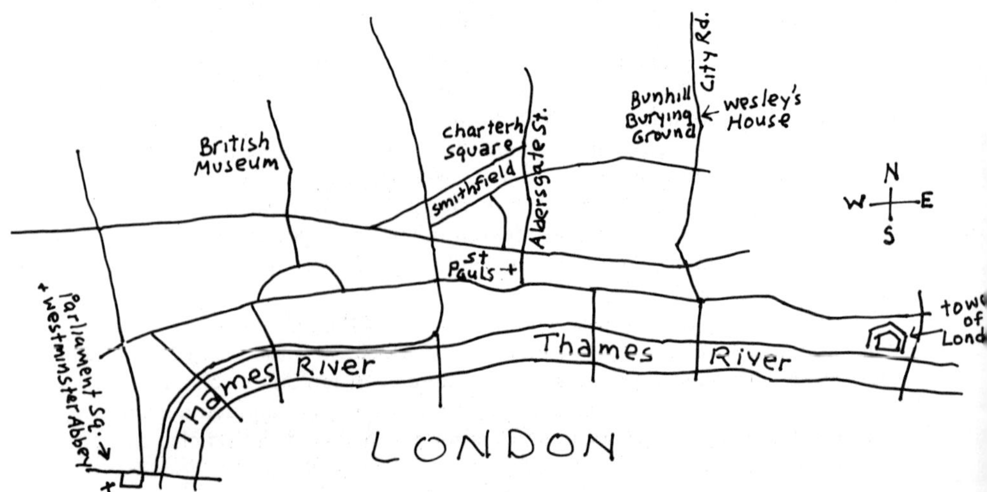

the 11th tablet of the Assyrian version of the Epic of Gilgamesh,
which records the Babylonian account of the flood (BM K3375)

a brick inscribed with the name and titles of Nebuchadrezzar II,
king of Babylon (BM 90081)

various statues of Rameses II, possibly the pharoah of the Exodus
(BM 67)

the celebrated Taylor Prism describing the campaigns of
Sennacherib against Hezekiah (BM 91032)

sculptured heads of Augustus Caesar (BM sculp. 1877), Tiberius
(BM sculp. 1881), Claudius Caesar (BM sculp. 1951-3-30,1) and Titus
(BM sculp. 1841)

There is also a small Palestine Antiquities room, which is a late addition.

4. The Wesley House and Chapel, and Bunhill Burying Ground, City Road,   IX-C
are two important nonconformist sites. John Wesley laid the foundation of this   IX-H
chapel in 1777, and often preached here during his later years. Adjoining the   VIII-D, N
chapel is Wesley's house, where he died in 1791. Part of the house is a museum.
Wesley is buried in the grounds at the rear. Across the road (which was built in
later times) is the Bunhill Burying Ground, the early graveyard for noncon -
formists. Susanna Wesley, mother of John and Charles, is interred here; also
John Bunyan, Isaac Watts, William Blake and Daniel Defoe. The grave of George
Fox is in the Friends Burial Ground nearby. See also

Plaques commemorating the conversion of the Wesley brothers on Little
Britain (Charles) and Aldersgate Street (John)

5. Hampton Court Palace and Windsor Castle, both a few miles up the River   XI-R
Thames from London, can both be visited in one day by Green Bus from Victoria
Coach Station or from Hyde Park Corner. They constitute two of England's most
important royal residences with considerable significance for the Christian
historian. The ornate red brick buildings and formal gardens of Hampton Court
originated with Cardinal Wolsey, who later found it expedient to present them to
Henry VIII. Here the drama of the official side of the English Reformation was
played out. In the magnificent state apartments Henry lived with five of his
six wives. The ghost of the unfortunate Catherine Howard is said to walk the
Haunted Gallery near the chapel where she made a last desperate attempt to
appeal to her husband. All the English monarchs from Henry VIII to George II
lived here. Hampton Court was also the scene of a conference called by James I
which resulted in the King James version of the Bible of 1611.

George's Chapel at Windsor Castle a few miles further up river is where
members of the English royal family have been interred since the 18th century.
The exquisite choir contains stalls for each of the members of the Knights of
the Garter, and Queen Elizabeth worships here on occasions. Windsor is the
largest occupied castle in Europe, and its state apartments are open to the
public (if you want to see how royalty lives). Some other sights of special
interest to Christians in and around London are:

VI-R   VI-S   VII-E   VIII-B   Charterhouse and Charterhouse Square just off the north end of Aldersgate Street, the remains of a Carthusian Monastery founded in 1371. The monks were cruelly executed at Tower Hill during Henry VIII's dissolution of the monasteries, and their brave end was witnessed from the Tower by Thomas More. Both Elizabeth I and James I stayed at Charterhouse for a short time at the beginning of their reigns. Later, Charterhouse became a school for poor boys, and included such famous members as Richard Lovelace, Roger Williams (founder of Rhode Island), John Wesley, the novelist William Thackeray and Lord Baden-Powell, founder of the Boy Scouts.

VII-D   Martyr's Memorial at Smithfield (on the wall of St. Bartholomew's Hospital across from the Smithfield meat markets). Notice the lovely half-timbered gate house of St. Bartholomew's Church nearby.

VIII-J   St. Giles Outside Cripplegate (in the Barbican not far from Aldersgate St., but since the bombing obscured by new blocks) where Milton is buried.

X-C   The British and Foreign Bible Society museum on Queen Victoria Street, containing many rare Bibles.

IX-F   George Whitefield's Memorial Church on Tottingham Court Road.

III-B   Lambeth Palace, residence of the Archbishop of Canterbury.

XII-A   Charles Spurgeon's Metropolitan Tabernacle (rebuilt) in Southwark.

VI-S   Chelsea Old Church, with a chapel built by Sir Thomas More.

VIII-J   John Milton's cottage near Chalfont St. Giles (in the western suburbs) where the poet finished PARADISE LOST while isolated from a plague raging in London.

VIII-N   The old Friends Meeting House at Jordans near Beaconsfield (also western suburbs) where William Penn is buried.

   Stoke Poges Churchyard, near Slough on the way to Windsor, where Thomas Gray wrote "Elegy Written In A Country Churchyard.

VIII-L   VI-S   St. Dunstan's In the West on Fleet Street, associated with John Donne and William Tyndale.

VIII-P   St. Paul's Cathedral, Ludgate Hill, built by Sir Christopher Wren after the Great Fire of London, and one of the most beautiful church buildings in the world. Wren's tombstone in the cathedral reads, "If thou seekest his monument look around."

London churches of historic interest are so numerous that it is not practical to list them all. At the City of London Information Center in St. Paul's Churchyard you can obtain a booklet called "London City Churches - A brief guide." Just two more are

St. Olaf's Church, where Samuel Pepys worshipped, according to his Diary, VIII-P and where the victims of the great plague of 1665-66 (some of them) are buried, IX-H and St. Mary Woolnoth Church on the corner of Lombard St. and King William St. near the Mansion House. John Newton, a former slave runner, was vicar here from 1779. Newton in turn influenced the great Christian statesman William Wilberforce who later was responsible for the abolishment of slavery by Great Britain.

Dr. Samuel Johnson's house off of Fleet Street on Johnson Court was the   X-C place where this remarkable man compiled the first English dictionary. Johnson was a friend of the Christian poet and educator Hannah More, and a genuine (though somewhat eccentric) Christian himself.

CAMBRIDGE

VI-B Cambridge has more associations with important events in the history of
VII-C evangelical Christianity than almost any other place in the world. John Fisher
VII-D (later Bishop) brought Erasmus to Cambridge, where the latter worked on his
VI-S Greek New Testament (1505-6, 1513-14). Around 1520 a group consisting of the
XI-E friars Robert Barnes and Miles Coverdale and university men such as Thomas
Bilney, Hugh Latimer, Nicholas Ridley and Thomas Cranmer, met at the
White Horse Inn to discuss the ideas of Luther. These men later became
England's chief Reformers. William Tyndale, England's first Bible translator
in the modern sense, studied at Cambridge. The preaching of Charles Simeon
at Holy Trinity Church led to the missionary commitment of Henry Martyn,
one of the early Bible linguists. Later, in the 19th century (1876), came the
establishment of the Cambridge Intercollegiate Christian Union, the meetings
of Moody and Sanky in 1882, the Cambridge Seven. From the late 19th century
onward Cambridge has produced a host of missionaries and has continually fed
evangelical men into the ranks of the Anglican Church clergy. When visiting
Cambridge see (not in order of importance)

V-F The exterior of the rooms above the gate to Queens College occupied by
VI-S Erasmus. John Fisher was master of Queens.

The site of the White Horse Inn (now occupied by the Cavandish Laboratory),

VII-B The portrait of Ridley in the hall at Pembroke College,

VII-D The pulpit used by Latimer in the church of St. Edward near the market,

VI-S, The portrait of Cranmer in the hall of Jesus College,
VII-D

Great St. Mary's Church, associated with several of the Reformers,

The Round Church (one of three round church buildings in England). This
and Holy Trinity are main evangelical churches near the university. St. Matthews
is another,

IX-G Holy Trinity Church with the memorial to Charles Simeon and the Henry
X-C Martyn Hall,

Kings College Chapel, breathtakingly beautiful, with the Rubens painting
over the altar,

XI-E Jesus Lane, where the early CICCU members pioneered a Sunday school,

XII-F Magdalene College, where C. S. Lewis was associated during the last years
of his life.

OXFORD
Oxford is Britain's oldest university, and it has had much to do with the history of Christianity in that land. John Wycliffe, John and Charles Wesley, John Henry Newman and C. S. Lewis are famous names identified with Oxford. Hugh Latimer, Nicholas Ridley and Thomas Cranmer were burned at the stake here under Mary Tudor. See especially

Balliol College, where Wycliffe was master in 1361, IV-C

Christchurch College, founded by Cardinal Wolsey. The Reformer John VI-S
Frith who assisted William Tyndale in his translation work and eventually was burned at Smithfield was a minor canon here,

Lincoln College was attended by John Wesley, and the Holy Club was IX-D
founded in his rooms in 1726. Other members were Charles Wesley and George Whitefield. The rooms, marked by a bust, were restored by American Methodists in 1928,

The cross in the center of Broad Street where the Oxford martyrs Latimer, VII-D
Ridley and Cranmer were executed,

The painting of Christ by Holman Hunt called "Light Of the World" in the chapel of Keble College,

The exterior of Magdalen College, where C. S. Lewis was a don. Lewis's XII-F
rooms were on the right, looking at the college from the back garden near the deer park. Lewis fans may also wish to see
The Eagle and Child and Lamb and Flag pubs on St. Giles St. where the Inklings group met,
Lewis's grave at Holy Trinity Church at the edge of town,
The Bodleian Library, which contains a large collection of Lewis manuscripts. Most of Lewis's personal library is now owned by Wroxton College, which uses the books for the study of English literature. The Bodleian Library will let visitors view manuscripts individually upon proper application.

CANTERBURY
"The Cathedral Church of Christ, Canterbury, is the Mother Church of III-B
Anglican Christendom, the cradle of English Christianity." So reads the opening VI-S
statement of a guidebook of Canterbury Cathedral. Associated with a number of Britain's most famous churchmen such as Augustine (the founder), Lanfranc, Anselm, Thomas Becket the Martyr (whose shrine was the most popular in England) and Thomas Cranmer, Canterbury Cathedral is still the seat of the Archibishop. The town of Canterbury itself, just a few miles southwest of London, contains much to attract the visitor. A good day trip from London by train, bus or automobile.

KNOLE AND PENSHURST PLACE

VI-S   Knole and Penshurst Place are two of England's great manor houses located in the county of Kent, just a few miles south of London. They are both exceedingly interesting for their architectural features and the dazzling wealth of their contents, and both have significant Reformation associations. The origin of Knole is lost in antiquity, but in 1456 it passed into the hands of Thomas Bourchier, Archibishop of Canterbury. From Bourchier onward it was held by four more archbishops, the last being Thomas Cranmer from 1532 to 1538. At this time Henry VIII often passed Knole on his way to Hever, the home of Anne Boleyn, and took a fancy to the place. He soon "persuaded" Cranmer to hand it over to him, but curiously enough did not spend much time there.

VIII-B   Penshurst Place, which contains one of the finest Medieval baron's halls left in the world, was presented to Sir William Sydney by King Edward VI. Its most famous owner was the poet Sir Philip Sydney, renowned for his Christian character and courtesy as a courtier of Queen Elizabeth.

       Both of these places can be reached by Green Bus from Victoria Coach Station.

THE WEST COUNTRY

       A number of English localities west of London in Alfred's old kingdom of Wessex hold special interest for Christian travelers. These include:

III-C   Winchester, King Alfred's fascinating ancient capital, also somewhat fan-
VII-D   cifully associated with King Arthur's Camelot. A statue of Alfred on horseback stands in the main street. The cathedral contains his casket, along with those of other Saxon rulers, but these remains were badly vandalized during the Civil War. Mary Tudor (Bloody Mary) was married here in 1554, and the chair in which she sat is on view along with other historical items too numerous to mention. Don't miss the grave of Jane Austin or the touching memorial to Isaac Walton (author of THE COMPLEAT ANGLER), a devout believer and biographer of George Herbert. Winchester can be visited from London on a day trip.

       Salisbury, a few miles west in Wiltshire, is also a quaint market town. Its cathedral has the highest spire in Europe (404 feet) and presents a breathtaking view as one approaches the town. The English painter Constable used Salisbury Cathedral as a subject many times.

I-A   Of equal interest to the Christian are the ancient pagan remains north of town called Stonehenge. This 4000 year old stone circle was most certainly used for religious rites, probably involving human sacrifice. Recent experiments have proven its incredible accuracy in predicting the point where the mid-summer sun will rise, plus other astronomical phenomena (authorities in recent times ring it with barbed wire at midsummer to keep off the modern pagans who throng there at that time of year and camp in the surrounding fields).

BRISTOL AND ENVIRONS

1. In Bristol itself, the most important evangelical landmarks are the "New IX-E
Room" (John Wesley's Chapel) and Charles Wesley's house. The latter can be
seen only from the outside (at 4 Charles St. near the bus station). Many of the
great hymns of the Christian church were written here. The John Wesley Chapel
is open to the public and a group can arrange for a free conducted tour. The
Chapel was built in 1739 near what was called The Horse Fair, and the Wesleys
preached here for some 40 years. From Bristol, Francis Asbury went out to
America in 1771 to found the Methodist Church there. See the unusual raised
pulpit, the great clock and the organ, all originals, and don't miss the museum
upstairs. Bronze statues of the Wesleys are outside.

In Bristol, see also the home of Hannah More, the Christian writer and edu- X-C
cational pioneer, at Fishponds. Hannah More also lived in a cottage built by XI-C
herself near the village of Wrington south of Bristol. She is buried in the churchyard there as is (somewhat ironically) John Locke the philosopher. The George
Muller homes still stand in Bristol, but are used by the city for educational
facilities and are not marked in any way.

2. Little Sodbury, some ten miles northeast of Bristol on the edge of the VI-S
Cotswolds, was for a time the home of William Tyndale, who was employed
here as tutor to the children of Sir John Walsh from 1521-23 after leaving
Cambridge. It was here that Tyndale formulated his plans for a translation of
the Bible into English from the original languages, at one time declaring to a
learned divine, "If God spare my life, ere many years, a boy that driveth the
plough shall know more of the Bible than thou doest." The church contains
Tyndale's original pulpit (rescued from a barn by the present vicar), and the
Manor House (open to the public upon application) retains much of its 16th
century construction and furnishings. See especially the garret where Tyndale
was housed. For a conducted tour and a very moving lecture on Tyndale's life,
parties may contact the vicar, Rev. Keith Ensor, telephone Chipping Sodbury
313 256. Lunches can be provided at moderate cost at the vicarage. This service
available Easter to September only.

3. South of Bristol, near Wrington, is a steep drive beside limestone cliffs IX-H
called Burrington Coombe. A plaque marks a cave-like slash in the rocks where
the Rev. Augustus Toplady (a contemporary and critic of Wesley) sheltered
during a thunderstorm and wrote the celebrated hymn, "Rock Of Ages."

III-C   4. Glastonbury, about 22 miles south of Bristol, has very early Christian
VI-R   associations, and is the site of a famous ruined abbey. Within the abbey, exposed
to the sky, is the spot where the high altar stood, which is marked. Pilgrims
often kneel in prayer there. According to legend, St. Joseph of Arimathea settled
on this spot to begin the preaching of the Gospel to England. He planted his staff
(or a piece of the Crown of Thorns) in the ground which grew into the famous
Glastonbury Thorn (still living, but obviously a much younger tree). The legend
is pure bunk, but the fact that a Christian community existed on this site before
the Saxon invasion, that the first Saxon abbot, Beorhtwald, was appointed here
about 670, that the abbey was plundered by the Danes and finally destroyed by
order of Henry VIII, makes it of considerable interest to the Christian historian.

THE MIDLANDS

XII-E   1. Coventry is the site of one of the most dramatic memorials in Britain to
the courage of the English people during the horror of the Blitz in 1940, and to
the staying power of the Christian church. The shell of the Old Cathedral stands
much as it was on the morning of November 15, 1940, after one of the most
devastating air raids of the war. Inside the ruin stands a simple cross of
charred timbers with the words "Father, forgive." Beside the ruin is the New
Cathedral, a completely unique modern creation, strikingly beautiful. Young
people from all over the world are on hand as volunteer guides during the
summer.

IX-H   2. Olney is a village on the main road from Oxford north to Northampton.
here, from 1764 to 1779, the curate of the 14th century village church was John
Newton, former slaver and renagade seaman (also associated with St. Mary
Woolnoth Church in London).In this village Newton befriended the poet William
Cowper, and the two collaborated on the OLNEY HYMNS, which include
"Amazing Grace," "O For a Closer Walk With God" and "There Is a Fountain
Filled With Blood." Newton is buried in the southeast corner of the churchyard.
Cowper suffered from manic depression and was cared for by Mrs. Unwin from
1767 to 1786 in a red brick house on the marketplace, now a museum.

XIII-D, N   3. The town of Bedford, about 50 miles north of London between Oxford and
Cambridge, is associated with John Bunyan, famous author of PILGRIM'S
PROGRESS and THE HOLY WAR. Bunyan lived in the village of Elstow just south
of town and there is a plaque on the cottage where he is thought to have resided.
His birthplace was at Harrowden one mile east. The church in Elstow has two
windows with scenes from Bunyan's stories. The Old Moot Hall contains a
collection of objects related to Bunyan including his father's will, which cut him
off with one shilling. The county jail and the lock-up on the Old Bridge where
Bunyan was imprisoned are both gone. The Bunyan Meeting in Bedford is built on
the site of the barn where he preached, and the bronze doors have scenes from
PILGRIM'S PROGRESS. The Bedford library and museum contain fine collections
of Bunyan relics and early books.

THE NORTH OF ENGLAND

1. The ancient city of York is one of the best preserved Medieval monu-   III-C
ments in Europe, and its great Minster is the largest of English Medieval cathe- III-N
drals. The Archbishop of York bears the title of Primate of England. York retains part of its original walls, and many of its streets are narrow and ir-
regular, lined with ancient buildings. From a Christian historical standpoint,
the Minster is the main place to see in York, and a proper visit will occupy at
least half a day. The first building on this site was a wooden chapel put up for
the baptism of Edwin, King of Northumbria, and his court by Paulinus, first
Bishop of York, on Easter Day, 627. The glory of the present building, begun
in the 13th and 14th centuries, is its magnificent stained glass windows, including
the largest sheet of Medieval glazing in the world (in the east window). To get
the most out of a visit to York Minster, buy a guidebook and do your own tour
or join one being given by a verger.

2. Durham, to the north of York, is the site of another splendid cathedral,   III-C
one that boasts the most striking situation of all English cathedrals on a raised
portion of ground on the bend of the River Wear. Begun in 1093, this great
Norman church houses the remains of St. Cuthbert (his shrine was destroyed in
1540) and The Venerable Bede. The chapter library contains the wooden coffin
of Cuthbert, illuminated manuscripts and a collection of early seals including
one of the Washington family. Don't miss the celebrated sanctuary door knocker,
a relic of the days when the cathedral was a place of refuge.

Visitors interested in The Venerable Bede may also drive a few miles
north to Jarrow where, in the monastery adjacent to St. Paul's Church (east
end of town), Bede was an inmate. His chair is on display. It was at Jarrow
that he died in 735.

3. Ripon Cathedral and Fountains Abbey in Yorkshire (northwest of the City   III-C
of York) are both significant remains of early Christian buildings in the north
of England. Ripon Cathedral is one of the smallest of the English cathedrals,
but it is one of the three original Christian centers in Yorkshire. It contains
the crypt of the Saxon Church of St. Wilfrid (634-709). The cathedral itself is a
fascinating combination of many styles and is famed for its wood carvings. Its
library contains a famous collection of early printed books including three
Caxtons. The town of Ripon retains the ancient custom of a "wakeman" or
watchman who blows his horn every night at 9:00 P.M. at the market cross.

Just four miles from Ripon is Fountains Abbey (which can be reached by car VI-R
or, for the more hardy, by public footpath), one of the largest and best preserved monasteries in England. The abbey is within the beautiful park of
Studley Royal through which runs the River Skell. It contains all the various
elements of a self-contained community, with buildings dating from 1135 to 1526
(at which time the abbeys were surpressed).

III-C   4. One of the oldest surviving church buildings in all of Britain is found not
far from Durham 3 miles outside of the mining town of Bishops Aukland. It is
the small and simple 7th century Church of Escomb.

EDINBURGH, SCOTLAND
        Edinburgh, the capital city of Scotland, lies along a ridge culminating in a
rocky eminence crowned by Edinburgh Castle. Descending from the castle to
Holyrood Palace are a series of interlinking streets called collectively "The
Royal Mile." The area adjacent to the "Royal Mile" comprises Old Edinburgh,
and all of the following top Christian landmarks are found here:

VII-I   1. Edinburgh Castle figures in the drama of the Protestant Reformation
VIII-B primarily as a dwelling of the ill fated Mary, Queen of Scots, and the birthplace
of James VI, later James I of England. The room of James' birth is on view.

VII-I   2. St. Giles Cathedral (the High Kirk of Edinburgh), founded about 1120 on the
site of an earlier church, is most famous for its first Protestant minister, John
Knox. Knox is buried at the rear of the church and the initials "I. K." in the
roadway mark the spot. In 1637 the bishop, David Lindsay, attempted to read
from Archbishop Laud's Scottish edition of the Anglican prayer book, whereupon one Jenny Geddes reacted by flinging a stool at his head. The wretched
bishop fled in a hail of missiles fired by the good wives of Edinburgh, and thus
began the public protest against English ecclesiastical domination which was to
result in the signing of the National Covenant the following year. The ultimate
result was the emergence of the national Presbyterian Church.

VIII-G   3. Greyfriars Kirk was the place where the National Covenant was signed in
VIII-O 1638. There is a memorial in the cemetery (northeast corner) to the Covenanters who died in the succeeding struggle.

VII-I   4. The John Knox House, at the lower end of High Street from St. Giles, was
lived in by the Reformer only the last three months of his life. He died here in
1572. The house is notable more for being a most picturesque survivor of the
16th century than for its historical significance.

VII-I   5. The Palace of Holyrood House, like the Castle, is most famous for its
VIII-M association with Mary, Queen of Scots. The Palace, which dates from 1500
(and looks very French in design), had its origin in the Abbey founded by David
I in 1128. The ruined nave of the Abbey is all that remains, and all that is left
of the original palace is the northwest tower associated with Mary. Here she
had her disputations with John Knox, and here her private secretary, David
Rizzo, was done to death before her eyes. Here also she married, first Darnley
and then Bothwell. Over a century later Charles II held court here for six weeks.
The adjoining State Apartments are occasionally occupied by the reigning

monarchs of Britain. (The one the Scots seem to appreciate most was the dissipated George IV, who in the early 19th century made a brief state visit and swathed his huge bulk entirely in tartans. His portrait graces the labels of various Scottish products.)

While in Edinburgh see also

Huntley House, an old time dwelling now a municipal museum containing many priceless historical items including the original Martyr's Monument from Greyfriars and the best copy of the National Covenant.   VIII-C

The Mercat Cross near St. Giles and the Grassmarket, where most of the public executions took place.   VIII-C

The various Closes (courtyards) along the Royal Mile, which sometimes have very interesting Biblical allusions over the entranceways.

DUMFERNLINE

Dumfernline, a short drive to the north of Edinburgh across the Firth of Forth Bridge, has a ruined abbey of considerable historical interest. It was built in 1072 by a Saxon princess, Margaret, who fled to Scotland in the wake of the Norman conquest. A chapel dedicated to her is in Edinburgh Castle. Margaret married Malcolm III, whose father Duncan, the first king of all Scotland, was slain by Macbeth. Benedictine monks lived here until its destruction by an English army in 1303. It was reconstructed by King Robert the Bruce, but again destroyed by the English in 1385. At the Reformation it was destroyed for good. Andrew Carnegie, who was born here, helped to finance its restoration in the 19th century.   III-G III-L

ST. ANDREWS

St. Andrews, Scotland's university town comparable to Oxford or Cambridge in England, is worth seeing for its present day charm and for its Reformation associations. Among other martyrs burned at the stake here was George Wishart, who profoundly influenced John Knox shortly after Knox's conversion. St. Andrews also has early Christian relics, including a sarcophagus of great rarity dating to the 9th or 10th century.   VII-I

ST. PATRICK'S IRELAND

The importance of Ireland's contribution to the evangelization of Europe cannot be overemphasized. There are many relics of early Christianity, but the important centers which flourished in the days of Ninian, Columba, Aidan and other great missionaries are pretty well wiped out. The major early sites have to do with St. Patrick.   III-B

Patrick, Ireland's patron saint, was from an historical point of view an evangelist of the first magnitude. No one knows where Patrick was born, but he was brought to Ireland as a young slave early in the 5th century. He ran away and eventually studied in France at the school of St. Martin in Tours. He was greatly moved to evangelize the land where he was enslaved, and in 432 landed on Ireland's east coast somewhere near Saul. Patrick's plan was to bring the people "by the net of the Gospel to the harbor of life." A special feature of his method was literature distribution, using copies of the Gospels and the Pentateuch. In 432, the year of his return, he met the High King and the Druids in a formal conference at the royal hill of Tara. Legend has embellished Patrick's memory with a great deal of nonsense, but he was nonetheless a great servant of God. Some important places associated with him are:

1. Armagh, where Patrick began his missionary work. Here are both the Church of Ireland and the Roman Catholic cathedrals, but neither building is of great antiquity. The public library possesses many priceless volumes of significance in the ecclesiastical history of Ireland including the fabulous Book of Armagh.

2. Downpatrick and its environs, on the coast south of Belfast is where Patrick first landed in 432 and where he is probably buried. The burial site is in the graveyard of Down Cathedral. The Abbey of Saul two miles northeast of Downpatrick is built on the site of a barn in which Patrick held his first Christian service. Near Saul on the top of a hill is a 35 foot high statue of the saint. At Raholp, two miles from Saul, there is a little ruined church, probably founded by Patrick. This is one of the oldest buildings in Ireland. Patrick is said to have received his last communion here.

VIII-R   3. The Boyne River Valley northwest of Dublin is the site of the residence of the high kings of Ireland who in ancient times dwelt in the Hall of Tara. Burial mounds of these kings are still to be found at Newgrange and other places in the Boyne Valley. Patrick is said to have lighted the paschal fire on the Hill of Slane in sight of Tara on Easter Eve, 432. According to the legend, the Druid priests prophesied to High King Laoghaire that if the fire were not extinguished at once it would never go out. Patrick, in fact, found Ireland pagan and left it Christian at his death.

The Boyne Valley was also the site of a great battle in 1690 when the Catholic forces of the exiled James II were defeated by the Protestant followers of William III of Orange, the stakes being the crown of England. Militant Irish Protestants have ever sence been called "Orangemen."

4. Two places of pilgrimage by Roman Catholics associated with St. Patrick are Croagh Patrick and Lough Derg. Croagh Patrick is the mountain near the County Mayo town of Westport where Patrick spent the period of Lent in 441. Here he is said to have banished the evil spirits from Ireland (and the snakes as well), thus defeating the evil forces of paganism. The traditional time of pilgrimage to the top now is August rather than Lent.

Lough Derg is a lake near the border town of Pettigo, and pilgrims spend three very rough days on Station Island in the lake. The tradition is that Patrick exorcized a demon who lived on the island and terrorized the inhabitants of that region.

IRISH CHURCHES, MONASTERIES AND CROSSES

The majority of the Christian landmarks to be seen in Ireland date from the 9th or 10th centuries onward. These consist of a host of picturesque churches, ruined monasteries and stone crosses. Fine sculptured crosses can be seen, for example, at Monasterboice (Co. Louth), Clonmacnoise (Co. Offaly) and Ahenny (Co. Carlow) in the northern part of the country. Examples of church buildings can be seen at Gallerus (Co. Kerry), Magnera (Co. Derry), Killeshin (Co. Carlow) and Ardmore (Co. Waterford), to name a few of the best early ones. Two well preserved monastic ruins are at Clonmacnoise and Glendalough (Co. Wicklow). Remains of later monastic communities survive at Holy Cross (Co. Tipperary) and Cong (Co. Galway).

Italy

Italy ranks second in importance only to Britain as a repository of Christian   I-A
historical landmarks in Europe. Rome, as capital of the Empire during the
Apostolic Age, soon developed a prominent Christian community. As the church
grew in size and influence, Rome became the capital of a spiritual empire
parallel to that of the civil government. During the Middle Ages, ecclesiastical authority radiated from Rome when there was no civil unity in Europe at
all. The Crusades were inspired from there. Many of the monastic orders were
born in Italy, and there the Renaissance first dawned. All of this had an impact
upon the environment in terms of architecture, art and engineering projects.
Thus to Italy, and especially to Rome, we must go if we are to gain any real
grasp of the visual history of Christianity in the western world.

ROME

While London is the chief city in Europe for post-Reformation Christian landmarks, Rome ranks highest in pre-Reformation Christian sights. Perhaps this is because Rome is the capital of world Catholicism and after the mid-16th century Britain became the stronghold of Biblical Protestantism with London as its center. For convenience, it is possible to divide the sights of Rome and its environs of special interest to Christians into four major areas:

1. Ancient Rome (most of which can be covered on foot starting from the   I-A
Piazza Venezia) includes the Forums, the Colosseum, the Arcs of Titus and   I-B
Constantine, Palatine Hill and so forth. The relics of Ancient Rome, built upon   II-A
the legendary seven hills, are so numerous that it is pointless to try to even
list them here. A good guide book (see A.2) such as Michelin's is an absolute
essential. Figure a minimum of one day to see much of Ancient Rome.

V-E   2. The Vatican City has two (or three) outstanding sights. These are
the great basilica of St. Peter's with its
grandiose Piazza, and
the Vatican Museum.

VI-C You can see both the Museum and St. Peter's in one day, but you won't see
much. Most guide books recommend being at the Vatican Museum when the
doors open at 9:00 A.M. and taking in the Sistine Chapel first. This is because
the guides leading tours are so noisy that it spoils the effect of awe that
Michaelangelo was trying to produce. The trouble with this plan is that the
Sistine is clear at the back and traffic is one-way through. The only way to
beat this is to see the Sistine ceiling, go through the rest, then start all over
again from the entrance. The paintings in the Vatican Museum are rivaled only
by the collections in Florence, and there are all sorts of other treasures besides.

St. Peter's is full of artistic splendors as well, not the least of which is
Michaelangelo's PIETA. What is thought to be the authentic tomb of St. Peter
has been discovered in excavations under the crypt in recent years.

3. The churches of Rome are numerous, but there are three within the city
aside from St. Peter's that every visitor to the Holy City should see. They are

St. John Lateran, founded by Constantine and officially the principal   II-B
church of the Catholic world. Nearby is the Lateran Palace on the site of
the first papal residence, and in a building facing the palace are the Holy
Steps, supposedly from Pilate's house in Jerusalem. You can watch pilgrims
earning indulgences by ascending the stairs on their knees.

Santa Maria Maggiore (St. Mary Major), founded in the 4th century by   II-C
Pope Liberius. The ceiling is gilded with gold brought back from the New
World by Columbus.

St. Paul Outside the Walls, thought to be built over the tomb of St. Paul.   I-B
Loyola established the Jesuit order here.

Some other churches of interest are

Gesù, where Ignatius of Loyola is buried,   VII-J

San Pietro In Vincoli (St. Peter In Chains). The chains are on view under   V-E
the altar, and this church also houses Michaelangelo's MOSES,

Santa Susanna's, the American National Church.

4. The Appian Way, the main highway of Ancient Rome outside the city to   I-B
the south, starts at San Sebastian's Gate. A half mile out is a small church
called the Quo Vadis where, according to legend, Peter met Jesus as he (Peter)
was fleeing the city and was moved to turn back and face execution. The cobble-
stones of the road, and the ancient statuary along the Appian Way are originals.
Near the highway are the catacombs, burial places of Ancient Rome where the
Christians met and found shelter during persecutions. The best known are

the Catacombs of St. Calixtus,

the Catacombs of St. Cecelia and

the Catacombs of St. Sebastian.

The bodies of Peter and Paul are thought to have been hidden in the latter.
Further out is the first century Mausoleum of Cecelia Metella, one of the best
preserved of ancient tombs in existence.

FLORENCE

Florence is the chief city of the Italian Renaissance, and all the main   V-E
Christian sights are either churches, palaces or museums containing the great
art treasures produced in the 14th and 15th centuries. In fact, the buildings
themselves in many cases are art treasures, and the whole city is a work of
art, particularly as viewed from the heights across the Arno River. The top
landmarks are

1. The Duomo (cathedral), whose huge dome designed by Brunelleschi   V-E
dominates the city. The dazzling white marble exterior with its mosaic designs
is an overwhelming sight. Across from the main building are the Campanile
(bell tower) and Baptistry, the latter with the famous bronze doors by Ghiberti.

V -F   2. The Palazzo Vecchio with its huge square tower was the political center of the Florentine government. It was here, in the Alberghettino Prison on the top floor, that Savonarola was tortured before being executed in the public square below.

V-E   3. The Ponte Vecchio, built in the 14th century, is the only one of Florence's ancient bridges left after the Germans retreated in 1944. There is an impressive memorial to this fact in the center of the bridge.

The most important museums in Florence are
V-E   1. The Uffizi Gallery, among the greatest collections of Renaissance paintings in existence. Buy a room-by-room guide book at the entrance and forget about time.

V-E   2. The Pitti Palace, across the Arno via the Ponte Vecchio, was the palatial home of the Medici family. Its collection of paintings rivals that of the Uffizi, and includes modern art as well. There is also a museum of silver. The palace and grounds are worth visiting just for their own sake. This all helps to create a context for understanding the Renaissance and its effect upon Christian history.

V-E   3. The Accademia near the Convent of San Marco houses Michaelangelo's glorious statuary, including DAVID.

III-M   4. The Laurentian Library in San Lorenzo, the church of the Medici, contains perhaps the most valuable collection of ancient manuscripts in the world (though this is difficult to evaluate).

V-F   5. The San Marco Convent has rooms decorated by the incomparable Fra Angelica. Savaronola lived at San Marco for ten years of his life.

V-E   Other churches which contain valuable Renaissance art are
San Lorenzo,   San Michele,   and Santa Maria del Carmine.
Santa Croce,   Santa Maria Novella,

MILAN

Milan is said by some authorities to be the third center for Renaissance
art in Italy. The two most important Christian sights are

1. Leonardo DaVinci's LAST SUPPER, painted on the refectory wall of the   V-E
Convent of Santa Maria delle Grazie. Exposure to the open air when the convent
was in ruins after the bombing of World War II caused considerable damage,
but the painting is still extremely powerful.

2. The gigantic Duomo, possibly the largest Gothic church in the world,   III-L
literally bristles with carved stone. It is a dramatic sight from the outside,
and the view from the roof is awesome.

Another worthwhile place to visit in Milan is

The Museum of the Pinacoteca Ambrosiana, which contains a large   V-E
collection of drawings by Leonardo DaVinci, an early Bible called the Codice
Atlantico and many fine paintings.

RAVENNA

In the face of the barbarian invasions, the emperors of Rome retreated to   II-A
Ravenna, and thus this city possesses some very early churches that reflect
this period in church history, as well as some very fine Roman remains. The
Mausoleum of the Empress Galla Placidia near the Church of San Vitale has
magnificent 5th century mosaics that are fine examples of Byzantine art. San
Vitale itself, and the old cathedral Sant' Apollinare Nuovo are also Byzantine in
style. The Basilica Ursiana is a Roman building that was later used as a church.
No student of early Christian art would want to miss Ravenna.

ASSISI

Assisi (in the hills near Perugia) is the birthplace of the beloved St.   III-I
Francis, and has one of the most beautiful settings of any city in Italy. It contains the great Basilica of San Francesco, which is a double church. The upper
church possesses Giotto's series of frescoes on the life of Francis. The Duomo
has the original baptismal font of the Saint. There is also a church dedicated to
Santa Chiara, a contemporary of St. Francis.

MONTE CASSINO AND SUBIACO

There are two sites in Italy associated with St. Benedict, the father of the   III-I
monastic system in the west. Benedict himself founded the monastery at Monte
Cassino in 529. It was very nearly destroyed by the Allied armies in 1944, but
has been rebuilt. Five war cemeteries are nearby. At Subiaco, just east of
Rome, there is the sole survivor of 12 hermitages set up under the direction of
Benedict. The first printing plant in Italy was established here in 1464. About a
mile away is the Holy Cave where Benedict lived for three years, located under
two churches. Here Benedict conceived his Rule for Monks, based on the motto
"Pray and Work."

Other places in Italy that may be of particular interest to evangelical Christian visitors are

VII-L   Trento (Trent), where the great Roman Catholic council met in the 16th century, partly to consider what to do about Protestantism. The cathedral and the Church of Santa Maria Maggiore where the Council of Trent met still stand.

I-B   Pompeii, near Naples, a Roman town wiped out by a volcano eruption in 79 A.D. and marvelously preserved. Here is what Roman life was like during the beginnings of Christianity.

I-B   Syracuse, in Sicily, was once the largest Greek city in the Roman Empire, and still has some splendid remains. St. Paul stayed here three days on his journey to Rome. There are catacombs here much larger than those near Rome that also have Christian associations.

III-A,J   Siena is Medieval Italy in all its splendor, preserved in its marvelous ancient buildings and streets, and in two festivals on July 2 and August 16 when the pageantry is incomparable - - and world famous.

III-A   Venice has a form of Christian art peculiar to its historical place as the Queen City of the Adriatic, and the gateway to the Far East in Medieval times. This is the spectacular Cathedral of St. Mark, a combination of African and East Indian styles. The city is filled with old churches, and there are several notable art museums.

Germany

Germany (West and East) has no one capital like London or Rome where Christian landmarks are most prominent. Rather, due to its history, it can be more easily divided into Roman and Medieval Catholic places, Protestant (that is, Lutheran) shrines and a few sites associated with the Hitler era, notably the memorials to atrocity victims.

ROMAN AND MEDIEVAL

II-B   1. Trier, on the Luxembourg border, is the oldest town in Germany,
III-I   boasting that it existed "1300 years before Rome." It was founded by Augustus about 15 B.C. St. Martin of Tours lived and worked here in the 4th century and Constantine the Great's father made his headquarters at this town. Helena,

Constantine's mother, brought to Trier among other relics from Palestine a coat supposedly worn by Christ, called the Holy Tunic. This is kept in the cathedral treasure and exhibited every 25 years. While at Trier see

The Dom (cathedral), oldest in Germany. It was first put up by Constantine the Great, and part of the walls are from the 4th century,   II-B

The Church of Our Lady, dating from 1235-1260, one of the oldest Gothic churches in Germany,   III-L

The Porta Nigra, a gateway fortress, finest Roman relic in Germany,   I-B

The Palace Gardens and Imperial Baths, built by Constantine,   II-B

The Roman civil basilica, one Constantine's throne room, much later a Protestant church. It has been rebuilt since World War II, and

The Rhineland Museum, with Roman antiques, and the Episcopal Museum with Christian relics.

III-D   2. Aachen, a few miles west of Cologne, was the capital city of Charlemagne's empire. The chief sight in Aachen is the Cathedral, the chapel of which was built by Charlemagne (hence the origin of the name of this town, "Aix-la-Chapelle"). The tomb of Charlemagne is under the dome. Thirty emperors were crowned in Aachen, and the coronation chair is on display. See also the 14th century town hall built on the site of Charlemagne's palace.

III-K   3. Cologne suffered much damage during World War II because of its location on the Rhine. The famous Cologne Cathedral with its dramatic twin spires was badly scarred (but, like St. Paul's in London, miraculously withstood the bombing when everything else around was flattened). It has been well restored. Cologne Cathedral had its beginnings when the Crusader Frederick Barbarossa brought back from the Holy Land the reputed remains of the "Three Wise Men" in 1164 and wanted a place for his relic to repose. The cathedral was more or less under construction for 600 years. Also worth seeing in Cologne are

I-B   The celebrated Dionysos Mosaic from the 2nd century, discovered during the excavation of a bomb shelter (chief among a number of Roman remains to be found in Cologne),

The Schnutgen Museum, which contains Christian exhibits, and the Roman-German Museum, which houses Roman finds,

The Church of the Minoriten, wherein is buried John Duns Scotus, the Scottish Franciscan and subtle theologian of the 13th century. This worthy has the distinction of giving to the English language the word "dunce" (because his intricate reasoning was hard to grasp).

PROTESTANT SHRINES IN EAST GERMANY
       All of the places associated with Luther's early life are in the German Democratic Republic (East Germany). They are accessible to the western visitor if one is careful to obtain the necessary visa and to follow the rules of entry. They include

VI-B   1. Eisleben in the Hartz Mountains where the Reformer was born, and where he died,

VI-B   2. Mansfeld, Luther's boyhood home town,

VI-B   3. Erfurt, where the Augustinian monastery in which Luther lived is now a museum. Luther's cell can be seen,

VI-C   4. Wittenburg, where the reconstructed Castle Church is located on whose door Luther posted the famous Ninety Five Theses. The Theses have been reproduced on bronze doors. Luther taught at the University of Wittenburg,

5. Leipsig, where Luther disputed with Johann Eck.   VI-D

While in East Germany see also the Nazi concentration camp of Buchenwald XII-D where 56,000 Jews and political prisoners died or were exterminated. Buses go from Weimar.

PROTESTANT SHRINES IN WEST GERMANY
1. The picturesque old university town of Marburg on the Lahn River (east   VI-H of Cologne, north of Frankfurt) was the seat of the Landgrave of Hesse. His castle, with the old town and the university sprawled below it, crowns a hill from which one can see the entire valley. In the castle, among other valuable exhibits, is the room where Luther and Zwingli met. William Tyndale also lived in Marburg for a time.

2. Worms, a town near the Rhine River where the Diet called by Charles V VI-F met, has a Luther monument near the old cathedral. The monument includes statues of a number of other Reformers as well. There is a plaque on the site of the building where the Diet was held.

3. Near Weinberg about ten miles from Heidelburg are the ruins of   VI-G Wartburg Castle where Luther translated the Bible during his exile.

4. The Diet Of Speyer where the Lutherans made their solemn protest in   VI-G 1529 is commemorated by a Neo-Gothic church called the Gedachtniskirche in the town of Speyer.

5. Augsburg has several associations with Luther and Lutheranism. In   VI-D 1518 Luther found refuge at the Carmelite monastery which was part of St.   VI-G Anne's Church, still standing. The Diet of Augsburg of 1530 called forth from the Lutherans the Augsburg Confession. In 1555, through the Peace of Augsburg, the Protestants won freedom of worship.

6. Coburg, in Bavaria, is the site of a fortress where Luther was detained   VI-F in 1530 under the ban imposed by the Edict of Worms. His room is on view.

OTHER IMPORTANT PLACES TO SEE IN WEST GERMANY
1. Munster was the site of the disastrous and fanatical Anabaptist uprising.   VI-I The cages used to exhibit the bodies of the executed leaders still hang from the   VII-M tower of St. Lambert's. The Peace of Westphalia signaling the end of the Thirty Years War was enacted in the Peace Hall, still standing.

2. The town of Constance on idyllic Lake Constance is where the Council of   IV-C Constance met which condemned the Reformer John Hus to death. See the Hus Museum in a former baker's shop where Hus stayed. The former Dominican

monastery where Hus was imprisoned is now a lakeside inn, The Insel. In the
building where the Council met there is a restaurant called (would you believe
it?) The Konzil.

XII-C,   3. Two shrines to victims of 20th century tyrannies are the Nazi concen-
D, H tration camp of Dachau outside of Munich, and the museum at the Berlin Wall
     near Checkpoint Charley. There is a Protestant chapel in Dachau.

Switzerland

III-B   Switzerland, the beautiful country of snow capped mountains and Alpine
     valleys and perhaps the world's most tourist-oriented nation was evangelized
     in the 7th century by St. Gallus, an Irish monk. Its most important contribution
     to the history of Biblical Christianity, however, occurred in the cities of Zurich
     and Geneva in the 16th century. Here the Reformed Church was born, and thus
     these two cities are of primary importance to the Christian visitor.

     ZURICH
VI-L   The great Romanesque church called the Gross Munster rises over the
     Limmat River at a point near where a Roman martyr, Felix, is said to have
     died. Its most famous pastor was the Reformer, Ulrich Zwingli. A statue of
     Zwingli stands near the bank of the river by the Wasserkirche just below the
     Grossmunster. His house is at the corner of Kirchgasse and Neustadtgasse
     and is now a kindergarten. Another place where he lived is at 13 Kirchgasse.
     Kirchgasse leads into the Zwingli Platz where the church is located. It has a
     severe interior and no altar, in keeping with the views of Zwingli. The crypt
     contains a 15th century statue of Charlemagne.

     Across the river is the Frau Munster with its imposing clock and steeple.
     This began as an abbey for the daughters of King Ludwig in the 9th century.
     According to legend, these girls saw a deer on the spot with lighted candles on
     its antlers. Like the Gross Munster, Frau Munster became Protestant under
     Zwingli and the adornments were removed. In recent years the Israeli artist
     Marc Chagall was commissioned to do five stained glass windows.

On the river banks a bit north (toward the railroad station) and across from the Grossmunster is a hill, on the top of which is a park where you can view all of the old town. This is the Lindenhof, and it was the site of the Roman and Celtic beginnings of Zurich.

The house of Conrad Grebel, Anabaptist leader who broke from Zwingli, is VI-J called "Zur Eintracht" House. It stands not far from the Grossmunster. Several of the Anabaptists were drowned in the river near the Wasserkirche as punishment for their heretical views.

The Swiss National Museum close to the railroad station has many articles on exhibit associated with Zwingli and the 16th century Reformers, including Zwingli's armor and sword.

GENEVA
Geneva is the city of John Calvin, the city that voted unanimously on May 21, VI-M 1536, to adopt the Reformation. Protestant refugees crowded into Geneva from VI-N all over Europe. Knox Knox was pastor to the English exiles, among them many VI-O scholars. The Geneva version of the English Bible was produced by them in 1560. Knox developed a church liturgy which became the basis for the order of worship of the Church of Scotland and of Presbyterian churches all over the world. Calvin remained in Geneva until his death, and is buried in an anomynous grave in the Plainpalais Cemetery. Things of Christian significance to see in Geneva are

The John Calvin Auditorium across from St. Peter's Cathedral (also known as the John Calvin Chapel or National Protestant Church of Geneva). This building was where Calvin and other Reformation ministers taught the Bible and Christian doctrine once a week to a group called the "Amateurs de la Sainte Evangile." It is now a Calvin museum, and English services are held on Sundays,

St. Peter's Cathedral is the church of Farel and Calvin. The only memento of Calvin here is his chair,

The Monument To the Reformation is in a park amid the remains of Geneva's 16th century ramparts. There are ten statues depicting Calvin, Knox, Farel, Beza, Admiral Coligny of France, William the Silent of Holland, Stephen Bocskay of Hungary, Friederich William of Prussia (who gave refuge to the Huguenots), Oliver Cromwell and Roger Williams. Various Reformation documents are depicted on the wall,

Calvin College, founded as the University of Geneva in 1558 and now a high school,

VII-G   The house of Agrippa d'Aubigné, Huguenot hero and poet, at 12 rue de l'Hotel de Ville.

IX-A   The Geneva Library (Bibliothéque) maintains in the Ami Lullin Room a permanent display of Reformation documents. See also the Jean-Jacques Rousseau Room with documents and mementoes of the father of modern liberal humanism.

THE CASTLE OF CHILLON

VI-L   On the opposite end of Lake Leman (or Lake Geneva) from the city of Geneva near the city of Montreux lies Chillon, one of the most picturesque and interesting castles to be found in Europe. Here Francois Bonivard, a Protestant preacher, was imprisoned by the Catholic Duke of Savoy from 1530 to 1536. His story (a highly fanciful version of it) was immortalized in a romantic poem, "The Prisoner of Chillon," by Lord Byron, who visited here in 1816. The castle dungeon furnishes a graphic picture of the brutality accorded religious prisoners. The column to which Bonivard was chained has Byron's initials carved into it. Chillon can be reached by Lake Steamers from Geneva or other points along the lake (which, incidentally, honor rail passes), a beautiful, leisurely trip.

ST. MAURICE-EN-VALAIS

III-I   St. Maurice-en-Valais is the site of a church built over the grave of a Roman legionnaire who was put to death for his faith. A monastery was established here in 515 where the monks became famous for their psalmody. Excavations have established St. Maurice as the oldest Christian site in Switzerland, dating to the 4th century, and the relics on view are highly interesting. The 6th century Ermitage de Notre Dame du Scex, accessible only by a rock hewn path, is still in use.

OTHER PLACES OF CHRISTIAN HISTORICAL SIGNIFICANCE

II-B   St. Gallen on the shores of Lake Constance is the site of the monastery
III-I   founded by St. Gallus (or St. Gall) in 612. The church of the former abbey, secularized under Napoleon, is now the most magnificent in Switzerland. St. Gallus is buried under the main altar. More important, perhaps, is the abbey library, which contains a fabulous collection of early church manuscripts.

The Monastery of St. Bernard with its famous hospice is located at the 8020 foot level of the St. Bernard Pass at Bourg St. Pierre. It became well known for its aid to travelers, and the monks still offer help to climbers in distress (and those dogs still carry brandy).

Ulrich Zwingli was born in the village of Wildhaus in eastern Switzerland,   VI-L
and his old wooden home is preserved. Zwingli was ordained a priest in
Constance and preached his first sermon at Rapperswil. He was a pastor in
Glarus for ten years.

In the city of Basle, the tomb of the great Humanist Erasmus is located in   V-F
the Munster.

Early Romanesque churches are still standing at Romainmotier village and   III-L
Payerne.

The Netherlands

The Netherlands, or Low Countries were, under Spanish rule in the 16th
century, one country. The name The Netherlands now refers only to Holland,
which became Protestant. Catholic Belgium has no major sights directly relating
to early Protestant history while Holland has many. Those associated with the
Pilgrim Fathers are of particular interest to Americans, and they are located
in Leyden and Rotterdam. Amsterdam, however, is most important in Reformation history.

AMSTERDAM
1. A good place to begin a tour of Christian sights if you have time is the
Amsterdam Historical Museum, housed in a beautiful 17th century building just
off the Kalvertstraat (the shopping street, closed to auto traffic). The exhibits
are organized to give you a chronological overview of Netherlands history including the Reformation period. If you just have a few hours, however, skip it
and go on to the primary sights.

2. Amsterdam has six churches dating to the 16th century or before: VII-F
the Old Church, the New Church, the Southern Church, the Western Church,
the New Lutheran Church and the English Church. The 15th century New Church
(Nieuwekirk) is beside the palace, and is Holland's royal church. It is the only
one generally open to the public. The English Reformed Church, however,
founded in 1607 (the same year Jamestown was founded), is located in the
Beguinage, a beautiful little park surrounded by 17th century houses, and is
the church of greatest interest to Americans and Canadians. Also in the

Beguinage is a Catholic "house church." The most impressive view of the other churches may be had in the evening when they are floodlit. They will be pointed out on a canal boat trip.

XII-E   3. The Jewish monuments of Amsterdam include the Portuguese Synagogue, Anne Frank's House, the Jewish Museum in the old weighing house, the house of the philosopher Spinoza and a statue called "The Docker" in a park near Spinoza's house. "The Docker" commemorates the general strike of February 25, 1941, in protest of the Nazi's treatment of the Jews. Most of these monuments in one way or another reflect the sufferings of the Jews over the ages.

4. The Bible Archeological Museum is a museum of exhibits related to Bible history, and includes a very fine model of the Israelite Tabernacle.

5. Amsterdam is the city of Rembrandt Van Rijn, and his memory is preserved here not only by the finest collections of his works in the world in the huge Rijksmuseum, but also by the Rembrandt House where other works and personal effects are on display. Rembrandt, who lived from 1606 to 1669, is honored as the greatest of all Dutch painters, and many of his famous works have a Christian theme, as follows:

> "Moses Descending From Sinai" (painting)
> "Pilgrims Of Emmaus" (painting)
> "Simeon In the Temple" (painting)
> "The Sacrifice Of Abraham" (painting)
> "The Woman Taken In Adultery" (painting)
> "Descent From the Cross" (etching)
> "Christ Healing the Sick" (etching)
> "Christ Presented In the Temple" (etching)
> "The Death of the Virgin" (etching)

Rembrandt is buried in the West Church.

6. "Our Lord In the Attic" Catholic Church near the Old Church is another "house church," a remainder from the early days of the Reformation when Catholics worshipped in secret. It is open to the public (for a fee), but still used for christenings, weddings and the like.

ROTTERDAM
This great harbor city was very nearly leveled by Nazi bombing. There are, however, still a couple of places of primary importance to Christian history, as follows:

VIII-C   The Pilgrim Father's Church, 21 Voorhaven, Delftshaven, in the harbor area, has stained glass windows depicting the Mayflower and the Speedwell.

The Pilgrim group gathered here to pray the night before returning to England and thence to North America in 1620. Nearby is a museum with a Pilgrim Fathers exhibit. The museum also features live crafts demonstrations.

The (reputed) birthplace of Erasmus of Rotterdam was destroyed in the   V-F
bombing, but the new city still honors him. There is a huge mosaic near the City Hall Square picturing him on a white horse. There is also a statue in a yard beside St. Lawrence's Church.

LEIDEN
The Pilgrim Fathers lived in Leiden during their stay in Holland and at   VIII-C
times attended St. Peter's Church. There is a plaque on the side of the church commemorating this fact. Nearby is a lovely group of early Dutch houses clustered around a garden which includes the residence of John Robinson, the English pastor. Robinson remained with his congregation in Holland after the Pilgrim group left for America. The Lakenhal Museum has two rooms devoted to the English Separatists.

HAARLEM
Many Christians (and others) who have read Corrie Ten Boom's THE HIDING XII-G
PLACE or seen the film will be interested to see the original hiding place of the Ten Boom family, The Beje. The address is
                              "Horlogerie ten Boom"
                              Barteljorisstraat lg
An English speaking guide is available at some times.

Belgium

Belgium has some of the finest Medieval remains in Europe and many, many ancient and beautiful Catholic church buildings. Two important ones are
The Cathedral of St. Bavon in Ghent, probably the greatest repository of church art in the country, including a magnificent altarpiece by the Van Eyck brothers, and
The Antwerp Cathedral, a gigantic building and one of the finest Medieval   V-E
cathedrals in Europe (begun in 1352). It contains three works by Peter Paul Rubens. Antwerp also has a museum of the art of printing, with the most complete antique press and engraving plant in the world.

V-F   The city of Bruges is said to be a living preservation of the Middle Ages, to Central Europe what Venice is to the South.

V-C   At Anderlecht just outside of Brussels there is a house once occupied by Erasmus of Rotterdam.

From a Christian historical perspective, probably the most important place to see in Brussels is the Museum of Ancient Art. It is divided into Renaissance paintings, Baroque art and Flemish Primitives. This is the best collection of Flemish Primitives in the world. (If you don't know what a Flemish Primitive is, buy a guidebook and find out.)

France

From the decline of papal power after Innocent III and particularly after the Great Schism, France remained politically aloof from the Vatican, yet never became Protestant as did Germany. The Protestants, or Huguenots, became numerous, but enjoyed only brief periods of tolerance. Thus there are only a few Protestant sights of great historical importance but many Catholic ones.

PROTESTANT MONUMENTS IN FRANCE

VI-M   There are two places closely associated with John Calvin. They are Calvin's (rebuilt) birth place at Noyon, 60 miles north of Paris, and

VI-N   The Protestant Church in Strasbourg, where Calvin was pastor for a time.

VIII-Q   Various sites in the Cévennes Mountains about 30 miles northwest of Nimes became places of refuge for the Hughenots after the revocation of the Edict of Nantes. The Protestant resistance lasted for about two years, 1702-1704, before it was crushed. This period is called The Desert, and there is a Museum of the Desert as Mas Soubeyran ten miles west of Alés. Nearby is a cave where the Protestants lived during the persecutions. Other Protestant memorials are to be found here and there in this area.

Catholic historical monuments are numerous, but the most important cities
are Paris and Avignon.

PARIS
1. The great Cathedral of Notre Dame on the Ile de la Cité has more asso-   IX-J
ciations with the mainstream of Christian history in France than any other
church. Paris itself began on this island, and Notre Dame, begun in 1163 under
Bishop Maurice de Sully, has figured prominently in the national life of France.
It has had whole books written about it (for example, NOTRE DAME OF PARIS
by Allan Temko, THE HUNCHBACK OF NOTRE DAME by Victor Hugo). In 1793,
during the Reign of Terror, the "Goddess of Reason" was set up on the altar.
Seven years later Napoleon was crowned here by the pope. The view of Paris
from its towers is unsurpassed.

2. Also on the City Island, entirely surrounded by the 13th century Palais
de Justice, is the incredible Sainte Chapelle, whose upper portion boasts an
array of stained glass that is absolutely unique. The scenes are from the Old
Testament.

3. Other significant Paris churches are:
The Pantheon on the Left Bank, whose great dome dominates the skyline.
Many of France's great figures of the last two centuries are buried here,
including Mirabeau, Voltaire, Rousseau, Victor Hugo and Emil Zola.
Rodin's THE THINKER is in this church.

St. -Pierre-de-Montmarte near Sainte-Chapelle is the oldest church in
Paris, begun in 1147. Two others from the same century are
      St. -Germain-des-Prés (1163) and
      St. -Julien-le-Pauvre (1160).

St. Germain-l'Auxerrois near the Louvre houses the bell that signalled   VII-G
the St. Bartholomew's Day Massacre of August 23-24, 1572.

St. Métard was besieged by Protestants on December 21, 1561.

St. Denis is where France's kings and queens are buried.

4. The Louvre, among the world's greatest museums, has a huge collec-   I-B
tion of Greek statuary including the WINGED VICTORY and the VENUS DI MILO   V-E
dating from Biblical times, and a great many Roman statues from the early
Christian era. Possibly its most famous possession is Leonardo Da Vinci's
enigmatic MONA LISA. There are works of art from just about every period.

5. The Bibliotéque Nationale has a wonderful collection of Medieval   III-M
illuminated manuscripts.

AVIGNON

IV-A   In the 13th century a series of popes resided in this city in the south of France. During the Great Schism that followed, Avignon was the residence of the Anti-Pope. The Palace of the Popes is a magnificent building with ramparts, built as a defense against bandits, that can be walked upon. The vast interior of the palace is a seemingly endless succession of chapels, cloisters and vaulted rooms.

I-B   Near Avignon are two important Roman ruins.
    Orange possesses a commemorative arch and the best preserved Roman theater in the world.
    Between Avignon and Nimes is Le Pont du Gard, a bridge and aquaduct with triple arches, marvelously intact after two thousand years. It is one of the most photographed landmarks in the country.

I-B NIMES

VII-G   Nimes dates to pre-Roman times and has some fine Roman ruins. It has been affected by all sorts of religious currents, but is most closely associated with the Huguenots who concentrated here during the Reformation.
    About 20 miles southeast of Nimes is Arles at the mouth of the Rhone.

III-D   This city was second only to Rome during the reign of Charlemagne.

III-K   Frederick Barbarossa received the royal crown of Arles in the cathedral here.

LOURDES
Lourdes is the most famous of a number of places in Europe where apparitions ostensibly of the Virgin Mary appeared to children. In this case the child, Bernadette, discovered a spring which is reputed to have healing powers. Tens of thousands of people come to Lourdes each year hoping for a miracle.

JOAN OF ARC LANDMARKS
The much romanticized story of Joan of Arc has its roots in genuine history. In the last stages of the Hundred Years War between France and England in 1452, the English had the French army bottled up in Orleans. A peasant girl who heard the "voices of the saints" urging her to expel the English and get the bastard Dunois crowned as king, Joan succeeded in firing up French morale. Under her leading they raised the siege, but a few months later Joan was captured, tried for witchcraft at Rouen and burned at the stake. She won in the end, however, because her martyrdom inspired the French leadership under the new king, Charles VII, and with the fall of Bordeaux in 1453 the English lost everything but Calais. Joan of Arc landmarks include

The house in which Joan was born in the picturesque village of Domrémy in Lorraine. The house is open to view and there is a museum nearby.

The Basilica of the Bois-Chenu at the southern outskirts of Domrémy is on the site of a tree where Joan heard the voices.

A reconstructed chapel at Vaucouleurs, 13 miles north of Domrémy, houses the statue of Notre Dame which was originally in a chapel at Bermont two miles north of Domrémy. There Joan went to pray before the statue each Saturday.

In Orléans, in the Cathedral of the Holy Cross, there is a chapel dedicated to Joan of Arc. Each May 7-8 there is a celebration of the deliverance from the English.

At Compigne near Reims is the tower where Joan was imprisoned after her capture.

A stone marker on the floor of the Vieux Marché (Old Marketplace) at Rouen identifies the spot where the young visionary was burned at the stake.

Spain

Inasfar as Spain does not figure prominently in the mainstream of Christian history from an evangelical perspective, it may be helpful to briefly review her background, which falls generally into seven periods since the time of Christ:

151 B. C. Becomes a Roman territory called Iberia or Hispania.
Christianity established throughout the peninsula in the 1st century.
5th-6th centuries The Visigoths, a Christian people, establish a powerful monarchy throughout the peninsula.
711 A. D. The Moors conquer the Iberian peninsula.
1479 A. D. Spain is united under a single Christian crown in Isabel, wife of Ferdinand of Aragon. The reconquest, led by the great orders of chivalry such as the Order of Alcántara, had begun in the 13th century. Columbus, with the blessing of Isabel and Ferdinand, discovers the New World in 1492.
1516-1700 Spain is ruled by the Hapsburg House of Austria. The Reformation occurs under the Hapsburg ruler Charles I, who becomes Charles V of the Holy Roman Empire in 1519. His successors are Philip II and Ferdinand I of the same family. The defeat of the "Invincible" Armada in 1588 destroys Spain's sea power.
1700-1902 Various wars and internal struggles, including the War of Spanish Succession with France (1702-14), during these two centuries strip Spain of all her European and overseas possessions, but leave her intact as a monarchy.
1902-present day The Civil War (1936-39) ends with Spain in the hands of a right wing Catholic dictator, General Franco. The combatants were known as the Red and the Black, the former being the Popular Front or Communists and the latter the Catholic National Movement. Franco was the final leader of the Black. Now, with Franco dead and the Communists still very active in the land, what will happen next is anybody's guess.

Being evangelized in the first century, Spain has been nominally Christian since the beginning, but the brief foothold gained by the Reformation was ruthlessly crushed by the Inquisition. The major Christian sights in this country, therefore, have to do with the struggle between the Muslims and the Christians or other phases of Spain's peculiarly Catholic history. They include

BARCELONA

The Tinell on the Plaza del Rey in Barcelona is the former throne room of the kings of Aragon where Isabel and Ferdinand greeted Columbus on his return from the New World. The entire square was originally part of the Royal Palace. A replica of the Santa Maria is tied up at the waterfront. Isabel and Ferdinand are known to historians as the "Catholic Monarchs." In one year of their reign, 1492, the colonial empire in the Americas was founded, the fall of Alhambra marked the defeat of the Moors and, under the Inquisition, the Jews were ordered to be baptized as Christians or leave Spain.

SANTIAGO DE COMPOSTELA

This city in the region of Galicia in Spain's northwest corner is a place of   I-A pilgrimage for Spaniards almost as important as Rome. Here, in the cathedral, rest the remains of the Apostle James the Great. James is thought to have accompanied Paul on the evangelistic mission to Spain after Paul's first imprisonment, and he too was beheaded under Herod upon returning to Rome. According to an early writer, his accuser repented, confessed Christ, and suffered martyrdom along with James. James's body was returned to Spain some time later. The shrine has been Spain's holiest site since Roman times, and has been defended against many enemies including England's sea raider, Sir Francis Drake.

GRANADA

In the southwest corner of Spain lies the beautiful city of Grenada, last   V-C stronghold of the Moors. Here can be seen the finest examples of Muslim architecture in Spain, including the world famous Calat Alhambra or Red Fortress. Here, too, is the Generalife, the summer palace of the kings of Granada, and the Chapel Royal, especially constructed by Isabel and Ferdinand for their final resting place. See the Michelin Guide for a summary of the many points of interest in this fabulous city, and Washington Irving's TALES OF THE ALHAMBRA for fuller background.

TOLEDO

This dramatic city just south of Madrid is one of Christendom's oldest centers (having had a bishop since the first century), and is now the primatial see of the Catholic Church in Spain. More familiarly, perhaps, it is the city of El Greco. Both its setting and its history are spectacular. It has had associations with the Romans, the Visigoths (whose capital it was), the Jews and, in the 1930's, the combatants in the Spanish Civil War. Main sights are the

The massive fortress of the Alcàzar,

The Cathedral (containing El Greco paintings),

The El Greco House and Museum, and

The El Trànsito Synagogue.

AVILA

VII-J   Avila is the city of St. Teresa, the 16th century Christian mystic who prompted spiritual reform within the Catholic Church during the time of the Protestant Reformation. A baroque chapel in the Convent of St. Teresa is on the site of the house where she was born. Avila is one of the highest cities in Spain (3670 feet), and was Christianized in the 1st century. A statue of Teresa dominates the main square. Teresa was a member of the Encarnación Convent of Carmelite Nuns for 27 years. beginning in 1535. This convent may also be visited. It has some objects on view associated with St. John of the Cross, another native of Avila. Teresa began her work of reforming the Carmelite Convents at St. Joseph's, also open to the public. She is entombed in the Carmelite Convent Church in Salamanca. Both Avila and Salamanca are easily accessible by fast train from Madrid.

Austria

Austria has been closely associated with Catholic Bavaria since early times VII-K
and derives its name "Osterreich" (or Eastern Realm) from this linkup. In the   VII-M
wake of the 16th century Reformation in Germany and Switzerland, a powerful
spiritual revival swept through Austria, and large numbers of people became
Protestants (estimated to be up to 90%). In a number of places the Catholic
church buildings became meeting places for Evangelicals (the word Evangelical
and the word Protestant are synonymous in Continental Europe). However, the
Counter-Reformation measures enacted by Ferdinand II in the 17th century for-
cibly returned the nation to Catholicism. Ferdinand, a descendent of Charles V,
was the first ruler of the Austrian branch of the House of Hapsburg (not to be
confused with Ferdinand I, brother of Charles V, who ruled over the eastern
part of the Holy Roman Empire after Charles stepped down). In 1619 Ferdinand II
became head of the entire Holy Roman Empire. His measures against the
Austrian Protestants began with banishment. Hundreds of thousands of Protestants left the country, but children under 14 were required to remain. Then followed the Farmer's War in which some 30,000 resisting farmers were killed.
Austria remained Catholic even after the Peace of Westphalia ended the Thirty
Years War, and today Protestants constitute only a small minority, mainly
Lutheran. Thus evangelical Christian sights in Austria are those associated with
the late 16th and early 17th centuries during the short Protestant period and the
persecution that followed.

PROTESTANT SIGHTS
The Landesmuseum in the castle in Linz contains one of the best collections
of Counter-Reformation historical items in the country. Throughout Upper
Austria there are still many reminders that this area had once been Protestant.
In particular, there are many Protestant memorials and historical markers, and
old Catholic churches often have a record of being at one time used by Protestants.

Schloss Klaus near the little village of Klaus (on the main road between
Liezen and Wels) is an ancient castle, parts of which date to the 10th century.
The owner of the castle, the Earl of Klaus, became a Protestant Christian during
Luther's lifetime. His descendent in the 17th century built a Protestant church
during the darkest days of the Counter-Reformation. Schloss Klaus today is a
Christian youth center training hundreds of Austrian young people in the Scriptures each year. The church still stands on the hill above the castle. It is possible to visit the church at any time and to see the castle from the outside. Permission to see the interior of the castle must be requested in advance by writing
to Mr. Peter Wiegand, Director, Schloss Klaus, A-4564 Klaus/Steyr, Austria.

CATHOLIC CITIES AND MONUMENTS

V-A   The city of Salzburg with its picturesque castle overlooking the town and the river and its ornate baroque buildings and fountains is the most popular summer tourist center in Austria next to Vienna. It has a unique Christian background. Founded in 700 by St. Rupert, it was soon made an archbishopric, and in the 13th century its bishops were given the title of Princes of the Holy Roman Empire. Three of the Prince-Bishops, Wolf Dietrich von Raitenau, Marcus Sitticus and Paris Lodron, were men of the Renaissance and created of Salzburg something of a "Rome of the North." Salzburg's greatest son, however, was Wolfgang Amadeus Mozart (1756-1791), whose almost unbelievable musical genius and life of triumph and tragedy are commemorated each year in the celebrated Mozart Festival. Many of Mozart's works including the last, REQUIEM, are of a Christian or religious nature. Mozart's birth house may be seen in Salzburg, but he is buried in a pauper's grave in Vienna.

III-N   Salzburg has two very old Christian sites, occupied now by Sts. Rupert and Virgilius Cathedral and St. Peter's Church. Both date to the foundation of the city when Christian buildings were put up on the ruins of the Roman town. The Medieval Mystery Play EVERYMAN is presented each summer during the Mozart Festival using the cathedral facade as a backdrop. St. Peter's is one of the oldest sites north of the Alps where Christian worship has taken place continuously. In the graveyard are catacombs that possibly were used by Christians in Roman times.

Hohensalzburg, the castle that overlooks the area and affords an excellent view, was the stronghold of the aforementioned Prince-Bishops.

In Austria's marvelously baroque capital city of Vienna, the two most important churches to see are the 8th century St. Stephen's Cathedral and St. Peter's (Peterskirche), possibly founded by Charlemagne. (Baroque, a style of architecture, horticulture and furnishings very evident in Austria and Bavaria, refers to the elaborately ornate - geometric forms, columns, scrollwork, domes, heroic Greek-type figures and all that sort of thing.) The top sight in Vienna, however, is the Hofburg, the imperial palace and residence of the Hapsburgs. This includes a number of magnificent places such as the Spanish Riding School, the Austrian National Library with some 36,000 manuscripts and 8000 early printed books, and the Castle Chapel. From September to June it is possible to get tickets to 6:00 P.M. high mass on Sundays when the Vienna Choir Boys perform.

V-C   Gratz in the southeast of Austria was a bastion of Christianity in the wars against the Turks. Vast quantities of arms were stored here to be distributed to volunteers whenever invasion seemed imminent. Today Gratz boasts a 17th century arsenal that was once the largest in the world and is now the only original one in existence. It contains 15,000 weapons of all kinds, a fascinating reminder that Christians were once called upon to physically defend their faith.

The Christmas carol "Silent Night" was first presented at a midnight Christmas Eve mass at the village church of Oberndorf about twelve miles north of Salzburg. The year was 1818. The carol was written by the assistant pastor, Father Josef Mohr; the music by the organist Franz Gruber. Gruber played it first on the guitar, however, because the organ had broken down at the last minute. A chapel dedicated to these two men now stands on the site of the original church. The house of Gruber is at Ansdorf two miles away, where he taught school. It is also kept as a memorial. Ironically, the origin of the carol was not discovered until 1854 when Father Mohr was already dead.

Greece

ATHENS

For the Bible believing Christian there is one site in Greece that is far and away the most important. This is the rocky outcropping below the Acropolis in Athens (just to the northwest) called the Areopagus, or "Mars Hill." To the right of the steps cut in the rock and ascending to its surface is a bronze plaque with the speech of St. Paul from Acts 17 in the Greek language. Below the Areopagus in a steep drop lie the recently excavated ruins of the Agora, or market place. At one end of this area is a beautiful replica of a stoa or public building (a contribution of Americans). In a far corner is the well preserved Temple of Vulcan.

The Areopagus and the Agora, with the stunning Parthenon crowning the summit of the Acropolis above them (a reminder that "God does not dwell in temples made with hands"), constitute the nearest it is possible to get in Europe to an original Apostolic setting. Corinth, Philippi, the Forum in Rome, the Appian Way, though impressive 1st century sites, pale by comparison. According to experts like E. M. Blaiklock, Paul actually made his address before a court held in one of the stoa that lined the market place. We know for a fact (Acts 17:17) that he argued with devout persons in the Agora. The sights that met his eyes as he glanced upward to the southeast are precisely those that will greet your eyes, despite a span of nearly 20 centuries.

OTHER CHRISTIAN SIGHTS OF SIGNIFICANCE IN GREECE

I-A   Corinth, about 50 miles along the coast from Athens, has well preserved
I-B   ruins of the Roman city established in 44 B.C. No physical description of
Corinth is given in the New Testament, so it is possible only to surmise what
Paul, Timothy, Silas, Apollo, Priscilla and Aquila might have seen of the relics
that remain.

The first three communities in Greece evangelized by the Apostle Paul are
in Macedonia on the northeast coast. They are:

Philippi, where the first European Christian congregation was established,
which has extensive ruins including a large Agora with many Roman buildings.
The traditional remains of the prison where Paul and Silas were incarcerated are
interesting but somewhat doubtful, historically, Here, too, are the river banks
where the "God fearers" met,

Thessaloniki, which now has nothing much in the way of 1st century remains.
However, it does boast some fine Byzantine buildings from the days when it was
the second city in the Byzantine Empire. A few Jews remain in the city from
among the thousands who came from Spain in 1492. These still speak a form of
early Spanish, and

Véria (Beroea), which also has nothing dating from the Apostolic Age.
However, the site of the synagogue where Paul preached is pointed out. A
ruined mosque is there now. Véria also has some small Byzantine churches.

In Apostolic times these Macedonian cities were linked by a Roman road,
the Via Egnatia, parts of which can still be seen.

Scandinavia

Scandinavia, the land of the fierce Northmen who ravaged Europe's coasts　VII-A
for centuries in their swift ships, was itself evangelized fairly late in western
history from other points in Europe. At the Reformation it became uniformly
Lutheran through religious leaders coming out of Germany. Most of the
Christian sights are early churches, including the famous Stave Churches,
although there are a few other memorials to the Scandinavian Reformers.
Christian visitors should also not miss the few remaining examples of Viking
ships which have been marvelously recovered from the bottom of harbors.

DENMARK
There are four churches of note in Copenhagen. They are　　　VII-A
The 17th century Vartov Church where N.F.S. Grundtvig, the great
19th century Danish preacher, hymnwriter and educator was pastor for 33 years.
The old Holy Ghost Church at Arnagertorv 22, part of Copenhagen's
"shopping street." This was established in 1296.
Grundtvig's Church, built in 1940 as a memorial. This is a remarkable modern style structure which resembles a pipe organ. Inside the entrance-
way there is the traditional ship model (to remind people to pray for their men
at sea) - - but that is the only thing traditional about it.
St. Ansgar's Cathedral, with relics of Scandinavia's first　　　III-H
missionary.

At Roskilde, a 20 minute train ride from Copenhagen, is Roskilde Cathedral where Denmark's kings and queens are buried. Nearby is the royal palace.
Also in Roskilde is a Viking Ship Museum possessing five of these remarkable　III-G
vessels.

Hillerod, 22 miles from Copenhagen, is where the unbelievably picturesque
Fredericksborg Castle is located. This former royal residence is a national
museum containing many reminders of Denmark's Christian background. The
chapel possesses a wooden organ built in 1634.

There are a couple of very important Christian sites on Jutland, the Danish III-H
peninsula which extends north from Germany. One is
The village of Jelling, where Denmark's oldest church building is
located, dating from the year 900, as well as the buriel mounds of Gorm the
Old and Thyra Danebod, Denmark's first king and queen. These mounds date to

950. Here are ancient rune stones, one of which was made by Harald Bluetooth, son of the above monarchs, who founded the church which stands there today (adapted from buildings already standing). Another Jutland place of interest is

Ribe, which like Bruges and Venice is a living relic of the Middle Ages. The cathedral is a beautiful 12th century combination of Gothic and Romanesque. The Priory of St. Catherine, founded in 1228, is the best pre-served monastery in Scandinavia. The post office was formerly the bishop's house. A third significant Jutland site, for good measure, is

Viborg, another great city of the past, which is associated with Hans Tausen, the "Danish Luther." Tausen was imprisoned in Viborg, but com-municated his radical ideas through his cell window. Upon his release he preached publicly in Viborg.

SWEDEN

VII-A   Stockholm, Sweden's capital city built on a network of islands, has two great churches of historical significance. They are:

The Cathedral (Storkyrkan), built in the 13th century, and containing some great works of art including a statue of St. George and the Dragon done in 1480. Olaus Petri, the Swedish Reformer, is entombed here. It is Sweden's royal church and is used for coronations.

The Riddarholm Church, which was originally built as a Franciscan friary in the 13th century. It is the burial place of Swedish kings.

Stockholm's Royal Library has a display of priceless books, including "The Devil's Bible," the Codex Aureus and the Revelations of St. Bridget.

Uppsala, just north of Stockholm, is the university town. Its cathedral is one of the most famous buildings in all of Sweden and has twin spires almost 400 feet high. It is the burial place of some of the nation's most illustrious people including Gustav Vasa, Sweden's first king. The university library, called Carolina Redviva, displays the 6th century Codex Argentus, a translation of the Gospels into Gothic. Two miles north is Old Uppsala, once the seat of pagan Viking kings. Three huge grave mounds date from the 6th century. Archi-ologists believe the ruins of a heathen temple lie below the 13th century church.

Sigtuna, on Lake Malaren between Stockholm and Uppsala, is the oldest town in Sweden and contains the ruins of the nation's first cathedral.

Visby, the capital of the island of Gotland, was a Viking trading center and the headquarters of the fabulous Hanseatic League some centuries later. It has ten Medieval churches still standing, and many ancient buildings. It is some-times called the "City of Ruins and Roses" (roses bloom there in November because of warm currents).

Two hundred miles north of Stockholm is beautiful Lake Siljan. The villages along this lake practice a variety of ancient customs that are a curious mixture of paganism and Christianity. Each village has a May pole which remains decorated all year long. In spring and mid-summer, dances are held in a rite that goes back before Christianity. Villagers still use (on occasion) church boats to row to services. Leksand and Rattvik have particularly interesting ancient country churches. A Bible based allegorical play is presented at Leksand each July in the open air.

NORWAY

Oslo became a cathedral city in the 11th century. The early buildings, how- VII-A ever, being made of wood, were destroyed by fires. The present cathedral building in Oslo is a combination of old and new.

The Old Aker Church is the earliest of Oslo's church buildings (1100), and has survived because it is built of stone.

While in Oslo, take the ferry to Bydgoy Peninsula to see the Viking Ship Museum (3 ships raised from Oslo fjord).

The Oslo City Hall contains a poignant mural depicting the suffering of the Norwegians under the Nazis.

Trondheim, on a fjord on Norway's northwest coast, was the capital during Viking times. The Viking king Olav Tryggvason replaced the pagan religion with Christianity in the 9th century, and is honored as a saint. In Medieval times Trondheim continued as the nation's capital, and even today Norway's kings are crowned there. Nidaros Cathedral (which uses Trondheim's early name) is built on the site of the saint-king's shrine, and was begun in 1150. It is the largest Medieval building in Scandinavia and Norway's most magnificent church.

Bergen, a colorful town on Norway's west coast, has a 12th century church, St. Mary's Church (Mariakirken), that has English services every Thursday evening during the summer. The baroque pulpit was donated by Hanseatic merchants in 1677.

Just at the outskirts of Bergen near Troldhaugen, the home of the composer Edvard Grieg, is the Fantoft Stave Church. These fantastic wooden structures dating from the late Viking era combine Christian and pagan symbolism. There are only about two dozen stave churches left in Scandinavia, primarily in Norway. This one was actually moved here from the Sogne fjord area.

FINLAND

The pagan Finns were evangelized in 1155 by St. Henrik, archbishop of VII-A Uppsala, together with the king of Sweden, in three campaigns (how about that for a Gospel team?). In the 16th century Mikael Agricola, the great Finnish Reformer, brought the country into the sphere of Lutheranism. Among other achievements, Agricola produced in Finnish a Biblical prayerbook, a translation of the New Testament from the Greek, translations of part of the Old Testament and the Psalms, and a church manual. Finland was under Swedish rule until the early 19th century, then ruled by Czarist Russia until its independence in 1917. It still has very close ties with the Soviet Union. About 93% of the Finns are nominally Lutheran, and a small percentage Orthodox.

In Helsinki, see Helsinki Cathedral on the north side of Senate Square, dominating the harbor. Inside the church facing the pulpit are immense statues of Agricola, Luther and Melanchthon.

See also Uspenskaia Cathedral, center of Orthodox worship. It can be recognized by its huge, bulbous onion-domed towers.

At Turku, Finland's second largest city, see Turku Cathedral, dating from the 13th century and the seat of the Finnish Lutheran Archbishop.

A few miles outside of Hameenlinna, birthplace of Jean Sibelius, is the beautiful Hattula Church dating from 1250.

ICELAND

VII-A   The center of early Christianity in Iceland is Skálholt. The tomb of Pall Jónsson, the most famous of the early bishops, is in the crypt of a modern memorial church at Skálholt. A visa is necessary for visitors to Iceland from the U. S.

Eastern Europe

With the exception of Hungary (East Germany, of course, doesn't count), the eastern countries of Europe have remained since the 17th century either Catholic (as in the case of Poland and Czechoslovakia) or orthodox until fairly recently. A few places in the border countries of Poland, Czechoslovakia and Hungary fall within the scope of this book because they have some relationship to the history of Christianity in Western Europe or to significant modern events. They are:

II-B
VII-M

PRAGUE

Prague is the city of Jan (John) Hus, the 15th century preacher whose reforming ideas pre-dated Luther. It is also a former capital of the Holy Roman Empire, and retains many monuments of its Medieval past. One nickname is "The City Of a Hundred Spires." The Old Town Square is a good place to start a walking tour. Here is the 14th century Old Town Hall with its incredible clock, complete with the 12 apostles and a bell ringing skeleton. Nearby is a huge statue of Hus. Across from the Old Town Hall is the Tyn Church, once a center of the Hussite activity. The two different towers represent "Adam" and "Eve." Take the street called Jilska and you will come to Bethlehem Chapel where Hus preached from 1402 until shortly before his execution at Constance. Also of Christian interest is the Jewish Quarter nearby with its Old New Synagogue (oldest in Europe) and cemetery. The memorial building to Nazi victims in the back corner of the cemetery has been closed, unfortunately.

IV-C

While in Prague, see also the beautiful St. Vitus Cathedral near Hradcany Castle (across the river from the Old Town Hall), and the famous Holy Infant of Prague, which is in the Church of Our Lady of Victory near the Charles Bridge. The Charles Bridge itself is a delightful remainder from Medieval times.

CRAKOW

Crakow is probably Poland's most interesting city from the standpoint of European history. It was not bombed as was Warsaw, and the old walled town within the city is remarkably preserved. Crakow is sometimes called the Polish "Rome" because of the many churches, especially in the old town. Kosciol Mariacki (St. Mary's Church), on a corner of the Old Market Square, with its uneven steeples, is perhaps the best known. Each noon an unfinished trumpet call is sounded from the taller steeple, a reminder of the Trumpeter of Crakow whose throat was split with a Tartar arrow as he gave the alarm.

XII-D   A few miles from Crakow is a 20th century place of pilgrimage, the grim
Nazi death camp of Auschwitz. Here some four million human beings were
systematically liquidated, with the aid of special ovens manufactured in Germany.
The statistics, which are so gigantic that they are difficult to comprehend, are
dramatized by whole rooms full, floor to ceiling, of shoes, eyeglasses, etc.,
left by just the very last transports of prisoners. The remaining gas ovens, into
which the bodies of the victims were thrust, are draped with flowers. Over the
entrance gate to the old camp is a sign which says in ghastly irony, "Work Makes
Freedom."

BUDAPEST

XII-H   Budapest (actually twin cities of Buda and Pest, like Minneapolis and St.
Paul) is a few miles down the Danube River from Vienna and can be reached
from there by riverboat. There is little of significance in the way of Christian
historical monuments in this Hungarian capital, but a must to visit is the re-
splendent Mattias or Coronation Church. It is on the hill overlooking the river,
and nearby is the Fisherman's Bastion which affords a marvelous view of the
city. This church is an official showplace, and occasionally a high mass by
Mozart or Haydn is performed on Sundays. The Catholic church of St. Stephen
the Martyr across the river near the central district is another show place. It
is generally full on Sundays. The seat of the Catholic primate of Hungary is at
Esztergom, where there is a large cathedral. There are groups of Bible
believing Christians meeting in cities like Budapest and Prague, but they tend to
keep a low profile.

GERMANY

POLAND

•Prague

•Krakow

CZECHOSLOVAKIA

AUSTRIA

•Budapest

HUNGARY

Portugal

Like Spain, Portugal's Christian history is pecularly Catholic, and goes   V-C
back to the same beginnings, being once the same country. 95% of the Portuguese
people are nominally Catholic. The nation of Portugal came into being under
Count Henry, a French crusader against the Moors, in the 12th century. After
defeating the Moors in a critical battle at Ourique, Henry was proclaimed king
in 1139. He established the seats of the two Catholic dioseses at Braga and
Coimbra. The monarchy lasted until 1910, and with the establishment of a republic political chaos ensued. 43 changes of government later, order was restored
with the emergence of Antonio de Oliveira Salazar as virtual dictator in 1932.
Religion was allowed by the constitution of 1933, but there was no freedom.
Salazar was followed by another dictator, Marcello Caetano, in 1968, whose
government was overthrown in a bloodless coup in 1974. At the moment there is
a leftist provisional government backed by a military regime. There has been
more religious freedom, but serious economic and political problems as well.
No one knows whether Portugal will continue as a NATO nation or veer off into
the Soviet orbit. There are no significant Protestant monuments in Portugal.
Some important Catholic places are found at the following centers:

LISBON
A monument to Portugal's great early-day Discoverers is on the river shore
between Lisbon's famous 3323 foot long bridge and the Atlantic. In the
Jerónomos Monastery just inland from the Monument, the first sea captain to
sail to India around the Cape of Good Hope, Vasco da Gama, is buried.

The Corpo Santo Church was founded by Irish Dominican friars in 1659,
who fled Ireland during the surpression perpetrated by Oliver Cromwell. It is
an Irish church to this day. During the religious crackdown in 1910, it was the
only Catholic church in Lisbon to stay open (thanks to British intervention).
St. Anthony's Church opposite the cathedral enshrines the house where the
Franciscan saint was born. There is also a huge monastery outside Lisbon
built by King John V to honor St. Anthony (who, the king felt, honored his
prayers for an heir).
Lisbon has the only church in Europe dedicated to the Sacred Heart. It is
the Estrela Basilica.

BRAGA
Braga has the oldest religious history in Portugal. Count Henry is buried in
the cathedral, which is built on the site of a Roman temple. A plaque from the
old temple is exhibited in the cathedral.

FATIMA

Fatima is a place of pilgrimage for Catholics near a village called Ajustrel. It is an isolated place fifteen miles from the railroad station which is called Fatima, but it draws tens of thousands of people each year. There is a paved esplanade which is eight football fields in length just in front of the shrine. In 1967 when Pope Paul VI visited Fatima, one million overran the area. All of this centers around a chapel which marks the spot where, on May 13, 1917, three children saw an apparition of the Virgin. Only one of the children survives today, Lucia, who is a nun at the Convent of St. Teresa in Coimbra. Altogether, there were six appearances of the Lady to these children, the last in the presence of 70,000 people. However, the children alone saw the apparition. Inspired by what he felt was a miracle of healing at the shrine, Father Harold Colgan, a pastor from New Jersey, founded a layman's organization called the Blue Army in 1947. The Blue Army has 27 million members in fifty-two countries.

SECTION C BIBLIOGRAPHY

PRIMARY SOURCES FOR THE CAPSULE HISTORY

Chadwick, Owen THE REFORMATION Pelican Books, 1964
A reasonably thorough one-volume paperback covering the main events of the Reformation and the reasons behind them.

d'Aubigne, J. H. Merle THE REFORMATION IN ENGLAND, vol. 2 Banner of Truth edition, 1963 (first written in 1866-78)
Very interesting look at events in England during the reign of Henry VIII in which the author differentiates between the political Reformation and the lesser understood spiritual movement behind it.

Douglas, J.D., ed. THE NEW INTERNATIONAL DICTIONARY OF THE CHRISTIAN CHURCH Zondervan, 1974
An absolute essential for historical reference, including people, places, movements, events, organizations, etc. Extensive bibliography. An expensive book ($24.95), but well worth it for anyone working with Christian history.

Durnbaugh, Donald F. THE BELIEVER'S CHURCH: The History and Character of Radical Protestantism Macmillan, 1968
This book traces the background and history of the non-conformist Christian bodies such as the Mennonites, German Pietists, Plymouth Brethren and so forth. Well written and authoritative, with extensive bibliography.

Latourette, Kenneth Scott CHRISTIANITY THROUGH THE AGES Harper Row, 1965
   "Here is an attempt to tell in brief compass the history of Christianity. " (from the author's introduction) In his longer works this distinguished author has dealt with the history of the Christian church, but here he attempt to show how "salvation history" and world history are really one and the same.

Littel, Franklin H. THE MACMILLAN ATLAS HISTORY OF CHRISTIANITY Macmillan, 1976
   This is a unique approach to giving a visual grasp of Christian history through the use of maps. A great help to understanding the geographical and territorial aspects of Christianity. Somewhat expensive book ($19.95)

Madden, Daniel M. A RELIGIOUS GUIDE TO EUROPE Collier Books, 1975
   This is obstensibly a guidebook, but the author includes quite a lot of useful religious history as well in a country-by-country format.

Moyer, Elgin S. WHO WAS WHO IN CHURCH HISTORY Keats Publishing, 1974
   A paperback reference book containing over 1700 brief biographies of the foremost personalities of Christendom.

Renwick, A.M. THE STORY OF THE CHURCH Eerdmans, 1958
   A brief work, but very useful in getting a handle on the main movements in Christian history. Inexpensive, interesting and easy to read.

ALSO RECOMMENDED

Bettenson, Henry, ed. DOCUMENTS OF THE CHRISTIAN CHURCH Oxford, 1963
   Valuable paperback reference book containing the texts of the most important Christian documents from the First Century to the Twentieth.

Latourette, Kenneth Scott A HISTORY OF CHRISTIANITY, 2 vols. Harper-Row, revised edition 1975.
   A synopsis of the entire scope of Christian history from the beginning to the present time. Has been described as something like a continuation of the book of Acts, which is a bit extravagant, but it is certainly the most complete history of Christianity in paperback.

Schaeffer, Francis HOW THEN SHALL WE LIVE? Revell, 1976. (also a study guide)
   This is a book about history and culture from a biblical Christian world view, the counterpart to a film series produced by Dr. Schaeffer and Gospel Films. A very thought provoking interpretation. It would enhance a visit to Europe as background for viewing Christian art and architecture.

Part Two
The Practical Side
of Christian Travel

SECTION A

THE
CHRISTIAN TOURIST

a. Some Basic Questions

b. Some Options

c. What Does A Self-Planned Trip To Europe Cost?

d. Laying Plans, Step-by-Step

e. Some Additional Possibilities

1. How To Plan Your European Pilgrimage

a. SOME BASIC QUESTIONS

There are a great many reasons why a Christian might feel justified in making a trip to Europe, even though the outlay in time and money is considerable. These range from the desire of retired persons to travel a bit now that they have the time and means to do so, to the adventurous urge of students to get away from their home environment and experience life in other cultures. Whether the trip fulfills any Christian purpose or not depends on some of the following considerations:

Do you have a goal for the trip that you can clearly commit to the Lord in the light of the costs involved?

What value will the trip have for others - - your family at home, your church, the people whom you will meet abroad?

In the long run, how will the visit to Europe contribute to your own spiritual growth?

How well prepared are you to make a trip abroad?
Do you know anything about European history or culture,
about Christian history in Europe or the current Christian scene?
Do you have any understanding of European geography, transportation systems, points of interest?
Do you have any special interests that you wish to pursue,
people whom you want to visit (for their sake, not just to get free lodging), places that you know something about beforehand?
How realistic are you about European currency, cost of hotels, meals, transportation?

This book is designed to help you ask, and find answers to, these basic questions. One way to start is by taking a look at some of the options open to you.

b. SOME OPTIONS

i NO PLAN OR PURPOSE AT ALL

There is something intriguing about obeying the existential urge to just take off for someplace. Many thousands of young people, in particular, are following the "call of the open road" and going abroad more or less without plan or purpose. The crowds hanging listlessly around public squares or huddled forlornly in railway stations are an indication that aimlessness is not all that romantic. The more fortunate wanderers with "contacts" hit the "address book trail," guided by the hopes of free bed and board with third cousins, friends of friends and missionaries (see A.8, Ethics). They are frequently rewarded by surprisingly cordial hospitality, often by Europeans who are only distant relatives of friends. It never occurs to them that they are taking gross advantage of a cultural phenomenon in Europe, that of the sacredness of providing shelter to strangers. The other side of that coin is the cost in time and actual money to these "contacts" who, for all practical purposes, are merely being used. A planless, purposeless trip to Europe can be a lark or it can be a bust, but the main question to consider is, Is it the best course for a Christian?

ii STUDY OR SERVICE ABROAD

These two possibilities are covered extensively in sections B and C.

iii A TRIP THAT IS PLANNED FOR YOU

There are various kinds of trips where the plans are laid by professionals and participants pay a certain stated price and climb on board. Two important choices in this department are package tours and people-to-people programs.

Package tours operated by American agencies, secular or Christian, have the advantage of being a quick, reasonably trouble free way to see a lot of things in Europe. Here are some samples taken from 1977 listings:

> Tour of France, Germany, Switzerland, Italy, Spain, Portugal.
> 15 days in April (off season). First class, most meals included.
> $1397.00 from New York (or $93.13 per day). Escorted.

> Tour of Scandinavia and the British Isles. August, 22 days.
> $1698.00 from New York (or $77.18 per day). Escorted.

The above are average priced, not expensive tours. They cover all transportation (except, perhaps, local carfare), room and board (note "most meals" - - not all), sightseeing arrangements, administrative details and leadership. They do not cover a multitude of incidentals - - no tour does - - but that cost is there just the same. It takes all sorts of services to make a package tour work - - the agent himself, the airlines, the local sightseeing tour operators, the hotel booking agencies, the bus operators and their drivers, etc. Naturally, the participant has to pay for all this convenience. Only certain kinds of hotels

and services are available to agents in this country, and these tend to be geared
to American pocketbooks.

Another more subtle factor, which could be positive or negative, is the
collective nature of a package tour. People in tours must travel in groups, and
many times this involves a group leader or several group leaders (sometimes
called "couriers.") The group and the leader can provide convenience and se-
curity on a tour. The foreign language ability of a courier is a tremendous help.
But traveling around with a group not of one's own choosing (numbering sometimes as many as 50 people), and being given the guided tour treatment day
after day can be an incredible drag.

People-to-people programs, mainly operated by secular organizations ,
are open primarily to students and young people, though experienced older
people can also take part as leaders. Generally, the plan consists of putting
Americans or Canadians in private homes in a foreign country so that they have
the opportunity of building a genuine human relationship. Oftentimes training
precedes the actual trip abroad. Besides the homestay, the program usually
includes some more extensive sightseeing, or perhaps some special activity
such as mountain climbing or youth hosteling. Costs run from around $1800.00,
all inclusive of the normal tour expenses, for seven weeks in Europe (based on
latest figures from The Experiment In International Living). The WHOLE
WORLD HANDBOOK (see A.2) contains lists of organizations specializing in
people-to-people programs. For specific information on three of the best known
ones, write to

> The Experiment In International Living
> Brattleboro, VT 05301
>
> AFS International Scholarships
> 313 E. 43rd St.,
> New York, NY 10017
>
> International Christian Youth Exchange
> 74 Liberty Place,
> New York, NY 10006

iv A TRIP THAT YOU PLAN YOURSELF

A single person, a couple of any age or a family can plan a meaningful,
low cost, highly interesting trip to Europe themselves. They can choose their
own traveling companions (two or three couples whose kids have grown up and
who enjoy one another's company make an ideal "group"), their own choice of
things to see, places and people to visit, and their own timetable. The key to
making one's own plans successfully is k n o w l e d g e - - that is, knowing beforehand what things cost, what accommodations are available and how to go
about booking them, how the transportation system works and, of course, what
there is to see and do in Europe. This book will help by supplying part of that

knowledge, and it will tell you about other inexpensive books and sources of information (section A. 2) that will cover the rest. The only thing that it won't do is help you to learn a European language - - that you have to do yourself, or get along without it.

c. WHAT DOES A SELF-PLANNED TRIP TO EUROPE COST?

Specifics on the basic costs of traveling in Europe are available in current secular guidebooks (see A. 2), and from tourist bureaux and travel agencies. However, here is a way to make a quick estimate of how much it would cost the average person to make a self-planned tour of Europe (obviously a student or young person - who get all sorts of price breaks - can get by cheaper, and a person used to going first class will spend much more):

LOCAL SIGHTSEEING TOURS - figure from $5. 00 to $10. 00 on the average for a two to four hour tour. Some cities, like London and Copenhagen, put on a municipal sightseeing tour, which is less expensive.

AUTO RENTAL - figure between $40. 00 and $50. 00 a week, plus gasoline (about $1. 50 to $2. 00 a gallon).

MISCELLANEOUS - figure that you will spend at least $3. 00 to $5. 00 a day for local transportation, entrances, guide books, post cards and postage, refreshments, and so forth.

ENTERTAINMENT AND SOUVENIRS - you should figure in a budget, large or small, for these two items. Most people like to take in a play, a circus or a cinema once in a while on their trip, and of course part of the enjoy- ment of travel is shopping for gifts. Entertainment will cost about the same for each event as a good meal. Gift items will cost about the same as they do at home.

MEALS - figure $2. 00 to $3. 00 for lunch, $3. 00 to $6. 00 for dinner. Generally, hotels and guest houses in Europe serve the large meal mid- day. Drinks are rarely included in the price of a meal, except breakfast. Unless specifically designated "English breakfast," this meal will consist of coffee or tea, bread, butter and jam in central and southern countries, with cheese and perhaps chocolate added in Holland. Some Scandinavian hotels include a buffet table with breakfast. An English breakfast consists of orange juice, egg and bacon, toast and marmalade, coffee or tea. Some people are able to get by on breakfast and one large meal when traveling, others cut down the cost by making picnic lunches.

TRANSATLANTIC FARE (See A. 4)

HOTELS - figure $12.00 to $15.00 per day for room and breakfast in cities for a tourist class hotel, or $15.00 to $20.00 for half-board (room, breakfast and dinner). Country places will cost slightly less, and costs will be higher in Scandinavia than in the south, but this is a good rule of thumb.

SURFACE TRANSPORTATION - this is a hard one to generalize on, because obviously it all depends on how often and how far you travel. For this reason, a tour or vacation that concentrates in a small area, say Ireland or Switzerland, is much cheaper than one that includes eight countries from Norway to Sicily. For a large group, the most economical way to get around is by bus (Europeans call them "coaches"), and this is true for individuals too, though the transport coach systems like Europabus are not nearly as convenient as the trains. For a small group, four to twelve people, the cheapest way is by auto or van (or mini-bus). However, most people find train travel in Europe to be the most satisfactory.

A simple way to figure the cost of 2nd class train travel in Europe is that it averages out to roughly five cents per kilometer. 1st class comes to roughly seven cents a kilometer. A round trip costs just about the same as a one way ticket. For example:

Luxembourg to Amsterdam 468 kms.
First class, one way - $30.00 (.06 per km.), round trip - $60.00
2nd class, one way - 20.70 (.04 per km.), round trip - 41.40

Luxembourg to Barcelona 1561 kms.
First class, one way - 96.70 (.06 per km.), round trip - 193.40
2nd class, one way - 65.60 (.04 per km.), round trip - 131.50

Luxembourg to Nice 1106 kms.
First class, one way - 97.00 (.09 per km.), round trip - 194.00
2nd class, one way - 64.90 (.06 per km.), round trip - 129.80

Luxembourg to Venice 985 kms.
First class, one way - 62.70 (.06 per km.), round trip - 115.80
2nd class, one way - 40.30 (.04 per km.), round trip - 74.20

Luxembourg to Oslo 1736 kms.
First class, one way - 163.10 (.09 per km.), round trip - 310.60
2nd class, one way - 105.80 (.06 per km.), round trip - 201.00

Inter-European air fares are at least twice that of the train.
It becomes quickly obvious, in the light of the above, that for people wish-
ing to do much train traveling in Europe, the rail passes are the best deal.
In 1977 they will cost:
   Student rail pass, 2 mos., 2nd class - $230.00
   Eurail Pass, first class, 15 days - 170.00
                        21 days - 210.00
                        1 month - 260.00
                        2 months - 350.00
Some countries, like Britain and Switzerland, also have their own rail pass
deals, which would be best if you were spending time just in that one place.

For students, there is an alternative to the rail pass. That is, making use
of special student rates on European trains and airlines (but only certain
trips). For information about 1977 schedules and how to book them, write
for a "Student Traveller" catalog to NUS Travel
                          Compass House,
                          Lypiatt Road,
                          Cheltenham, Glos., England
Send a couple of international postal certificates for a quick reply.

d. LAYING PLANS, STEP-BY-STEP

To start planning your own tour of Europe, here is what you need:
   This book
      One or two of the recommended general guidebooks
         Possibly a special guidebook, such as the YHA guide or the
         Eurail guide.
   A good, large map of Europe, possibly a road atlas.
      Sightseeing aids - maps and brochures from tourist bureaux,
      Michelin Green Guides, etc.
         Some figures from a travel-agent on the current air fares
   A list of people you want to visit, places you "must see," etc.

From these resources, you can arrive at these vital ingredients:
      An itinerary - - perhaps loose and flexible if you are footloose
      and fancy free, or fairly tight if you are on a limited time schedule.

      A budget. By using the above guidelines, try to take everything into
      account. Be realistic - - figure that you will spend m o r e than you
      think. If it works out the other way around, great!

      A list of hotels, resorts, etc., where you plan to stay. It is smart
      to book ahead, especially if there are several of you in a party,
      unless you want to be v e r y flexible.

A plan of what you want to do and see in each place. Don't make the
mistake of waiting until you get there. It is very easy to lose sight
of your purpose once you arrive on the scene, and to end up just
hanging around the hotel or looking in store windows. On the other
hand, it is good to plan some "unplanned" days just to rest up.
Try to make Sundays special, and to join with other Christians if
possible. Try also to keep a daily devotional life.

Here is a sample plan for a very pleasant four week pilgrimage-type
European vacation for a couple. It covers a lot of ground and yet allows time
for relaxation and a change of pace from sightseeing. Being designed to concen-
trate on a particular subject - Christian history - it does not attempt to "do"
all of Europe or even all of the main tourist attractions in the places that it
touches on. Prices are approximate.

APEX fare, Chicago-London-Rome-Chicago (summer season)	$625.00
7 nights in a tourist class hotel, London, including English breakfast, figuring $25.00 per couple	87.50
Local transportation, entrances and miscellaneous	21.00
Round trip bus journeys to Cambridge and Canterbury	6.85
Train and ferry to Hook of Holland	30.00
Eurail Pass, first class, 21 days, to begin on day of arrival in Holland	210.00
4 nights in tourist class Amsterdam hotel, incl. breakfast	50.00
Day trips to Leyden, Rotterdam using Eurail Pass	n.c.
Train and ferry to Copenhagen using Eurail Pass	n.c.
3 days in Copenhagen Mission-Hotel incl. breakfast	37.50
Day trips to Lund, Sweden, and Fredericksborg	n.c.
Train and ferry to Cologne, Germany	n.c.
3 nights in Cologne hotel, incl. breakfast	37.50
Day trips to Marburg, Aachen	n.c.
Train to Gwatt, Switzerland	n.c.
6 days in Reformed Church resort on Lake Thun, full board, @ 15.00 per day	90.00
Day trips to Geneva, Chillon, etc., including lake steamers	n.c.
Train to Rome via Milan	n.c.
5 nights in Rome tourist class hotel, half board @ 20.00	100.00
Day trips to Naples and Pompeii, Subiaco	n.c.
39 meals @ 4.00	156.00
Local transportation, entrances, etc., on the Continent	63.00
TOTAL	$1514.35

This works out to $54.08 per day, and there is no
scrimping. Furthermore, miscellaneous expen-
ditures are included. Entertainment and gifts, of
course, are an additional expense, as they
would be at home.

Here is another sample self-planned tour, this time for three weeks. This
time the economics are based on two couples (though figures are quoted per
person.) Again, prices are approximate. The trip is figured as from the West
Coast.

TGC, Oakland-London-Oakland(high season)	$429.00
7 nights in London hotel, including breakfast	87.50
3 day-trips on bus to Hampton Court/Windsor, Cambridge and Canterbury	9.25
Local transportation, entrances and misc.	21.00
Two week auto rental, unlimited mileage	100.00
Gasoline (based on 750 miles)	50.00
Ferry to Calais, round trip	35.00
Drive to Paris	——
2 nights in Paris hotel incl. breakfast	25.00
Drive to Gwatt, Switzerland (near Thun and Interlaken)	——
8 nights in Swiss Reformed Church resort, full board	120.00
Drive to various points of interest in Switzerland	——
Drive to Strasbourg	——
1 night in Strasbourg hotel, bed and breakfast	12.50
Drive to Reims	——
1 night in Reims hotel, bed and breakfast	12.50
Drive to Dunkirk	
1 night in Dunkirk hotel, bed and breakfast	12.50
Ferry to Dover, drive to London	——
1 night in London hotel, bed and breakfast	12.50
26 meals @ 4.00	104.00
Miscellaneous expenses on the Continent	30.00
TOTAL	$1108.25

For two people, this comes out to $1033.13
each, or $49.20 per day. (Actually it is less
than that, because the transatlantic flying
time is not counted.) For four people, it
would work out to $995.50 each, or $47.40
per day.

Just by rule of thumb, the longer the tour the less the cost will be per day,
simply because the price of transatlantic fare is spread out over more days.
The total cost, of course, would be much less if one were to cut down the time
and the scope of travel. For example, a couple could spend two full weeks in
Britain, say one week in London and another at a Christian guest house in the
Scottish Highlands, do day trips from London, rent a car for a week and drive
all over the north of Britain and come out at just about $50.00 per day or $1400.
for the two of them, total. A similar plan for Switzerland would work out just
about the same.

Now that you have the basic facts of how to go about a self-planned tour, the next step is to put pencil to paper and start laying plans. To do this, however, will entail some further information about what certain guidebooks can do for you, what the transatlantic air fare scene is like in 1977 and what choices are open to you in terms of Christian places to stay. These subjects will occupy the next few sections.

e. SOME ADDITIONAL POSSIBILITIES

Before we leave this section on planning, however, I would like to suggest that there a r e other, even less expensive ways of touring Europe or enjoying a vacation there. These include:

RENTING A CAMPER OR MOTOR HOME
   See A. 2 for sources of information about vehicle rental.

CAMPING OUT
   See A. 2 for a guidebook on this subject, and for sources of information.

YOUTH HOSTELING
   See A. 2 for guidebooks and sources of information.

A BICYCLE TRIP
   The following person is a Christian worker who organizes bike trips for evangelicals. You don't have to be young (or v e r y young, anyway). Write to Mr. Don Dunlap, "Unterwegs," Ortsstrasse 60A, 7842 Kandern 5, Germany.

A PACKAGE VACATION THROUGH A BRITISH AGENT
   There are in Britain several Christian travel agencies offering very economic and unusual package vacations. The main drawback to these deals is that they are, of course, geared to British people, whose life style and way of looking at things is just a w e e bit different from ours. However, if you think you can cope, they do sound pretty neat. One agent, in fact, tells me that he is commencing to advertise in the U. S.

The Holiday Fellowship, 142-144 Great North Way, Hendon NW4 1EG, England. (tel. 203-3381) This outfit features "Holidays That Are Different," including hiking in many parts of Britain, plus vacation programs featuring painting, music, sailing, archaeology, photography, bird watching and just about about anything else that a person could take an interest in. My favorite is "Life In a Cloister," a week spent visiting and studying various Medieval monasteries in the north of Britain (complete 1977 cost including room and board, about $85. to $95. 00). Write for a free catalog.

The Country Wide Holidays Association features package vacations all over Britain and every part of Europe from Lappland to Sicily. The emphasis is on nature and the open air. Their address is
Birch Heys, Cromwell Range, Manchester M14 6HU, England (tel. 061/224-2887)
Catalogs available if you are seriously interested.

Raymond Cook Holidays also has package vacations at attractive prices throughout Britain and Europe. Holy Land tours are offered as well. Write for a catalog to 25 High Street, Dover, Kent CT16 1ED, England (tel. Dover 204404)

2. Guidebooks and Information Sources

Just about anything you need to know about traveling in Europe has been written down by somebody. Most of the essential information about transportation, hotels, restaurants and so forth are in certain guidebooks. You can get a lot of help from tourist bureaux in some of these areas as well, and especially some good sightseeing materials.

The bibliography that follows contains what I consider to be the best guides, written by people who have been in the busines for a long time. Most of the material is checked periodically, and thus is reasonably reliable.

Unfortunately, the cost of books is rising rapidly, and the 1977 prices in some cases aren't available yet (at the time of this writing). Therefore, the price I quote and the one you will find on the latest edition may be different.

a. PRACTICAL GUIDEBOOKS

Practical guidebooks are the ones that give all the lowdown on how to get to Europe, how to get ready to get there, what life is like when you get there, and extensive information on surface transportation, hotels, meals and other items of expense. They also contain some sightseeing material. I recommend:

FIELDING'S LOW COST EUROPE Temple Fielding, Fielding Publications, 4.95. (Fielding's TRAVEL GUIDE is more extensive - and expensive)

EUROPE ON $10.00 A DAY Arthur Frommer, Arthur Frommer, Inc., 4.95. (Frommer also has DOLLAR-WISE GUIDES to individual countries, but this one has the "mostest for the leastest.")

FODOR'S EUROPE UNDER 25 Eugene Fodor, David McKay Co, 4.95. (Despite the title, an excellent practical guide for anyone.)

LET'S GO: EUROPE Harvard Student Agencies, 4.95. (A book published by a student organization, but containing good practical information for everyone.)

b. STUDENT GUIDEBOOKS

WHOLE WORLD HANDBOOK, Marjorie Cohen, Council on International Educational Exchange, 2.95. As the subtitle says, this is "a student guide to work, study and travel abroad." It is the best popular book on this subject available - - a gold mine of resources, addresses, advice, etc.

YOUTH HOSTELER'S GUIDE TO EUROPE, Youth Hostels Association, Collier Books, 2.95. Covers 22 countries. "How to go, what to see, where to stay - on a budget." Gives details on walking, cycling tours and backpacking. 60 maps and charts.

c. SPECIALIZED GUIDES

THE EURAIL GUIDE: HOW TO TRAVEL EUROPE BY TRAIN, Marven Salzman and Kathleen Muileman, Salzman Co., 5.95.

ENJOY EUROPE BY CAR: EVERYTHING YOU NEED TO KNOW ABOUT DRIVING ABROAD, William J. Dunn, Scribners, 5.95.

A RELIGIOUS GUIDE TO EUROPE, Daniel Madden, Collier/Macmillan, 4.95. Has some good introductory information on the religious background of various countries, but padded out with reams of irrelevant stuff.

d. SIGHTSEEING GUIDES

Britain and Ireland

BLUE GUIDES (England, Ireland, Scotland, Wales, London), Rand McNally, 9.95 each. Thorough and excellent.

WARD LOCK'S RED GUIDES (covers every area of Britain and North Ireland in individual books), Ward, Lock, Ltd. Around 3.00 to 4.00 each. Also thorough and very good guides. Not generally available in the U.S.

HOLIDAY GUIDES (individual books on England and Ireland) Random House, 2.95 each. Put out by Holiday Magazine. Small, very attractive format with lots of pictures, clear text. Not too detailed.

The Continent

MICHELIN GREEN GUIDES (every part of France, plus Austria, Germany, Italy, Portugal, Spain and Switzerland) Michelin Tyre Co., 4.95 each. Beautifully and logically organized, with maps, drawings, time lines, diagrams, historical summaries, etc.

BLUE GUIDES (Northern and Southern Italy, Rome, Northwestern and Southern France, Paris, Southern Spain, the Bernese Oberland and Lucerne, Denmark, Greece and Athens. Rand McNally, 9.95 each.

HOLIDAY MAGAZINE GUIDES (Italy, Rome, France, Paris, Scandinavia, the Low Countries) Random House, 2.95 each.

FODOR'S GUIDES (covers most European countries) David McKay Co. Generally 9.95 to 10.95 each.

e. THE NATIONAL TOURIST BUREAUX

Each country in Western Europe maintains one or several tourist offices in the U.S., and upon request will send sightseeing brochures, maps and specialized information. The East European nations also have information offices, sometimes in connection with their consulates or trade missions, and will send visa forms and other data about touring. Here are addresses of the main tourist offices:

Austrian National Tourist Office, 545 Fifth Avenue, New York, NY 10017
      630 Dorchester Blvd., Montreal, Quebec
      401 Bay Street, Box 21, Toronto, Ontario
Belgian Tourist Information Office, 720 Fifth Avenue, New York, NY 10019
British Tourist Authority, 680 Fifth Avenue, New York, NY 10019
      151 Bloor Street W, Toronto, Ontario
Czechoslovak Travel Bureau (Cedok), 10 E. 40th St., New York, NY 10016
Danish National Tourist Office, 75 Rockefeller Plaza, New York, NY 10019
Finnish National Tourist Office, 75 Rockefeller Plaza, New York, NY 10019
French Government Tourist Office, 610 Fifth Avenue, New York, NY 10020
      1170 Drummond Street, Montreal, Quebec
German Democratic Republic, 400 Madison Avenue, New York, NY 10017
German National Tourist Office, 630 Fifth Avenue, New York, NY 10020
Greek National Tourist Organization, 601 Fifth Avenue, New York, NY 10017
MALEV, Hungarian Airlines, 630 Fifth Avenue, New York, NY 10020
      Hungarian Embassy, Consular Division, 7 Delaware Ave., Ottawa
Iceland State Travel Office, 505 Fifth Avenue, New York, NY 10017
Irish Tourist Board, 590 Fifth Avenue, New York, NY 10036
      2100 Drummond Street, Montreal 107, Quebec
      7 King Street E, Toronto, Ontario
Italian Government Tourist Office (ENIT), 630 Fifth Ave., New York, NY
      3 Place Ville Marie, Montreal, Quebec   10020
Netherlands National Tourist Office, 576 Fifth Avenue, New York, NY 10036
      Suite 3310, Royal Trust Tower, Toronto-Dominion Center, Toronto
Norwegian National Tourist Office, 75 Rockefeller Plaza, New York, NY10036
Portuguese National Tourist Office, 570 Fifth Avenue, New York, NY 10036
Spanish National Tourist Office, 122 E. 42nd Street, New York, NY 10017
      13 Queen Street E, Toronto, Ontario

Swedish National Tourist Office, 75 Rockefeller Plaza, New York, NY 10019
Swiss National Tourist Office, 608 Fifth Avenue, New York, NY 10020

f. INFORMATION SOURCES
Air Tickets From London Onward
Christian Travel International Ltd., Drayton House, 30 Gordon Street,
London WClH OAN, England   387-5280

Bus Fares and Routes
Practical guides, national tourist bureaux and
EUROPABUS, 630 Fifth Avenue, New York, NY 10020

British Rail Tickets (including ferry tickets across the Channel)
BritRail Travel International, 270 Madison Avenue, New York, NY 10016
or any travel agent.

Camping In Europe
Practical guidebooks, national tourist bureaux and
AAA World Wide Travel, 1712 G St. NW, Washington D.C. 20006
The AAA can issue the necessary membership for using European camp-
grounds (10.00 to join in 1973). They also publish a camping and caravaning
atlas that would be a must for this activity.

Inexpensive Train Tickets From London To Continental Points
Trans-Alpino office in Victoria Station (east side). These bargains are
limited to students of any age and young people under 21.

Rail passes
Any travel agency, the French National Railroads (610 Fifth Avenue, New
York, NY 10020) or national tourist bureaux (for special train deals within
particular countries).

Railroad Timetable
A Continental Timetable book is available from Thomas Cook travel agents.
It gives railroad timetables all over Europe including the USSR, the Near
East, North Africa and North America. Purchase from any Thomas Cook
office in England or get an application form from a Thomas Cook agent in
the U.S. or Canada. The Eurail Guide also has some timetables.

Renting an Auto, Mini-bus or Camper
Consult the practical guides, ENJOY EUROPE BY CAR, or write to national
tourist bureaux for lists of agencies (England and Holland are the best
places to rent from). If you want to buy a car in Europe, there are agencies
in North America that can help you, possibly your local dealer. Check the
practical guides and look in your local yellow pages.

3. The Transatlantic Air Fare Situation

The most economical way to get to Europe, in terms both of time and of money, is to fly. Flying across the Atlantic is often the largest item in one's travel budget, but it is possible to save up to one half of what it c o u l d cost by doing a bit of research and advance planning. In fact, in most cases advance planning is the main prerequisite for getting in on the less expensive air fares. Here is a run-down of the cut rate types of air fares to be offered in 1977:

AFFINITY CHARTERS. These are offered by large business firms, universities, travel clubs and other such organizations. You have to have been a member in good standing of the sponsoring organization for at least 6 months before you can book a seat on an affinity charter. You are required to book seats on one particular charter going and returning, and if the block of seats does not fill up, they cancel and return your money. The problem is that sometimes cancellation does not take place until it is too late to get any other advance booking deals. There is a slight saving over the TGC. For example, the British American Club price for a 30 day affinity charter, Oakland-London, June 10 to July 10, is $376.50, and the TGC price is $429.00.

TRAVEL GROUP CHARTERS. For the TGC's you don't have to be a member of a group or sponsoring organization. Instead, you have to sign up and pay a significant part of the price 65 days in advance of the flight. You can't change your mind without losing money. TGC's are set up by commercial organizations like Char-Tours and often use space on scheduled airlines such as TWA or Pan American. They are advertised through brochures which most travel agents will have. However, some agents, especially in university areas, specialize in cut rate air fares and will have the most complete information. Your deposit is protected by being placed in escrow but, as with the affinity charters, you do take a risk in that if the TGC falls through it is often too late to save money on anything else.

ONE-STOP TOUR CHARTERS. OTC's offer a package deal for people interested in going to one place like London, Paris or Madrid, having a week or two
of theaters, night life and rubbernecking and having everything pretty well arranged beforehand. If you can use the whole package, then the price is compar-
atively cheap as package tours go. For example, TWA offers a two-week
theater package in London and Paris which includes all sorts of goodies - -
airport transfer, 6 theater performances, several sightseeing tours, free
"membership" to gambling casinos (watch that one), "discounts" at various
shops and restaurants (another hooker) - - but only Continental breakfast and
no other meals. The price tag for May is $798.00 from New York, or $57.00
a day.

YOUTH FARE. Youth fare is not the least expensive of the promotional or
economy fares, but it has several advantages if you qualify. (To qualify you
merely have to be under 22 years of age.) One is that it is good for up to one
year. This means that a student wants to take a six or nine months course in
Europe, he or she can use the youth fare ticket round trip while all other promotional fares would not allow enough time. The second advantage is that it is
not necessary to sign up in advance. The fare is the stand-by type, so seats
can not be booked until three days before the flight. Furthermore, the passen-
ger can choose the airline, flight time, etc., and can also change his mind
about the return flight. It has the "open jaw" provision, meaning that one can
fly in to one city in Europe and out from another. Being standby, if the plane is
full they bump you.

THE APEX FARE. The APEX is an excursion fare, and you have to stay
away from 22 to 45 days. Also, you must sign up two months in advance and
pay in full. However, unlike a charter, the APEX allows you to select your
airline, flight, destination, etc., on both legs of the trip. It has the "open jaw"
provision, but no stop-overs.

EXCURSION FARE. Regular excursion fare does not require advance signup. There are two kinds of excursion fares, 22-45 day (the least expensive) and
14-21 day. Both cost more than the APEX fare.

ICELANDIC AIRLINES. Icelandic does not belong to the International Air
Transport Association (IATA) and thus can offer slightly lower fares than the
other scheduled airlines flying the Atlantic. The best deal is from New York or
Chicago (their only U.S. ports) to Luxembourg. Low season APEX fare on
Icelandic, NY-LUX, is $325.00, regular APEX from NY to Geneva $370.00.
However, the train connection between Luxembourg and Geneva would cost
another $30.00.

round trip

summer season	from LA/SF	from CHI	from NY
Youth fare - London *	$696.00	$572.00	$546.00
APEX - London	593.00	491.00	460.00
APEX - Geneva	657.00	555.00	505.00
22-45 Excursion-London	755.00	648.00	592.00
Regular Fare			
to London	1148.00	994.00	826.00
to Geneva	1264.00	1042.00	894.00
* Youth fare may be subject to a 10% increase in 1977.			
ALL FIGURES ARE APPROXIMATE AND NEED TO BE CON- FIRMED.			

HOLD EVERYTHING!

A new arrival in the "alphabet soup" of air fare packages as this book goes to press is the ABC (Advance Booking Charter, which may modify everything I've said above.) The trouble is, while TWA and PanAm confirm that the ABC is indeed coming for summer 1977, nobody has any details. The ABC, according to an article in this week's TIME Magazine, will require only 45 days advance signup, only a week's minimum stay in Europe, and is even cheaper than the TGC. TIME gives this example of a round trip fare, NY-London in summer 1977:

ABC	$300.00 to $389.00
TGC	379.00
APEX	460.00

4. Christian Hotels, Guest Houses and Hostels

There are, in Britain and Continental Europe, a great many Christian hotels, guest houses and hostels. Some of these places are conventional hotels, others are like big houses (which they were, formerly), farms which are still being worked or vacation spots which some Americans would call "resorts." Most serve meals, in facilities ranging from complete restaurants to small dining or breakfast rooms. They are great places for getting to meet European Christians, and generally they give very good value for the money. Most are in the "moderate" range - - $7.00 to $12.00 a day for full board. They must be booked directly, and are not available through agents in this country or abroad.

Obviously, the choice of these places depends much on your personal interests, itinerary, plans, budget, etc. Also, the status of hotels tends to shift, particularly in these times of inflation and unstable currency. Therefore the number one rule is - - WRITE AHEAD FOR CURRENT INFORMATION (or, if you are in Europe, phone). (Most of the specific listings given in this book are based on information published in 1974, 1975 and 1976 - - 1977 information is just now available.) When you write, enclose a couple of international postal certificates for an airmail reply. For many of the Christian hotels, advance booking of from 6 months to a year is advisable. However, if you decide at the last minute, it would be worth your while to make a phone call.

Note to young people: some of these places engage extra help during the summer, but the compensation would be more in terms of experience than in money. Apply early and send references.

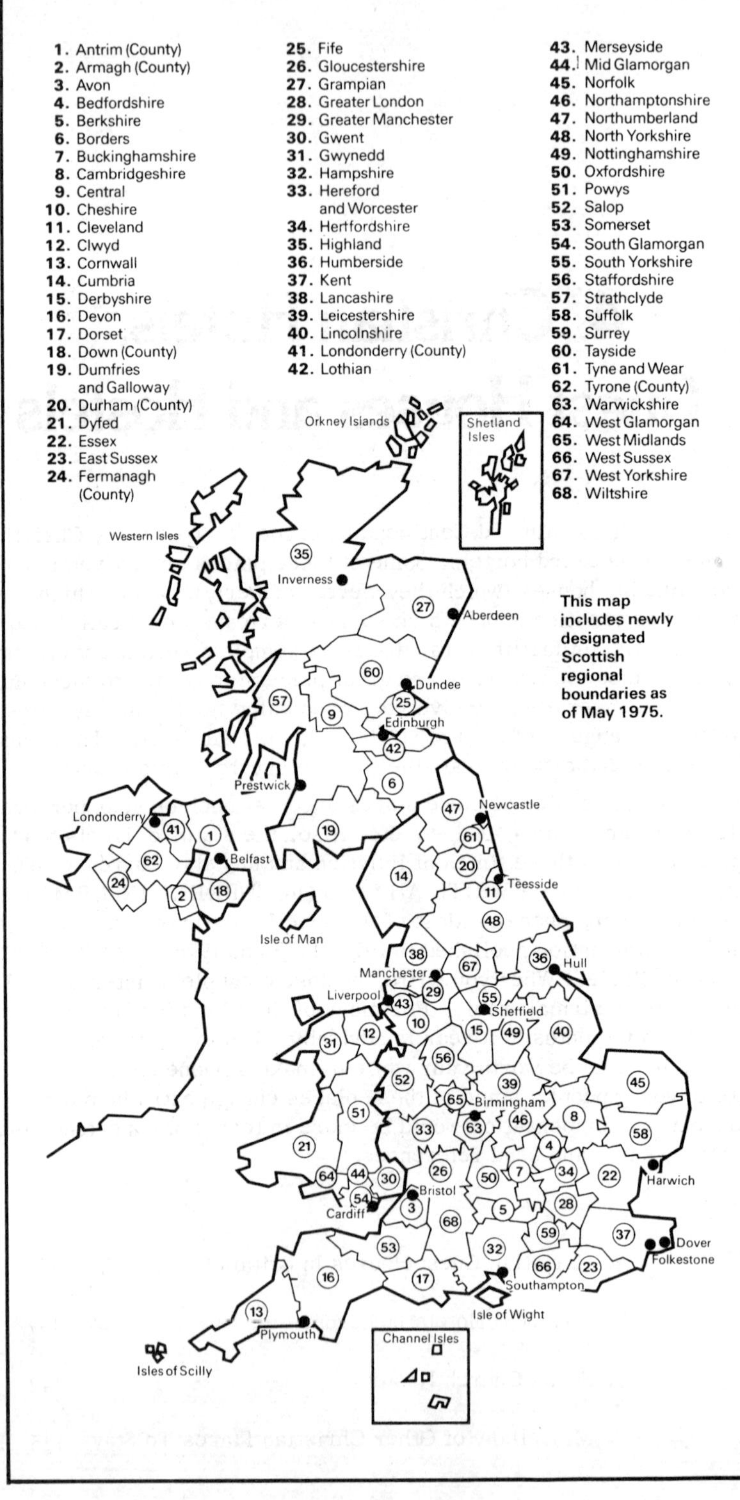

1. Antrim (County)
2. Armagh (County)
3. Avon
4. Bedfordshire
5. Berkshire
6. Borders
7. Buckinghamshire
8. Cambridgeshire
9. Central
10. Cheshire
11. Cleveland
12. Clwyd
13. Cornwall
14. Cumbria
15. Derbyshire
16. Devon
17. Dorset
18. Down (County)
19. Dumfries and Galloway
20. Durham (County)
21. Dyfed
22. Essex
23. East Sussex
24. Fermanagh (County)
25. Fife
26. Gloucestershire
27. Grampian
28. Greater London
29. Greater Manchester
30. Gwent
31. Gwynedd
32. Hampshire
33. Hereford and Worcester
34. Hertfordshire
35. Highland
36. Humberside
37. Kent
38. Lancashire
39. Leicestershire
40. Lincolnshire
41. Londonderry (County)
42. Lothian
43. Merseyside
44. Mid Glamorgan
45. Norfolk
46. Northamptonshire
47. Northumberland
48. North Yorkshire
49. Nottinghamshire
50. Oxfordshire
51. Powys
52. Salop
53. Somerset
54. South Glamorgan
55. South Yorkshire
56. Staffordshire
57. Strathclyde
58. Suffolk
59. Surrey
60. Tayside
61. Tyne and Wear
62. Tyrone (County)
63. Warwickshire
64. West Glamorgan
65. West Midlands
66. West Sussex
67. West Yorkshire
68. Wiltshire
Orkney Islands
Shetland Isles
Western Isles
This map includes newly designated Scottish regional boundaries as of May 1975.
Inverness
Aberdeen
Dundee
Edinburgh
Prestwick
Newcastle
Teesside
Londonderry
Belfast
Isle of Man
Manchester
Liverpool
Sheffield
Hull
Birmingham
Bristol
Cardiff
Harwich
Dover
Folkestone
Southampton
Isle of Wight
Plymouth
Channel Isles
Isles of Scilly

a. Christian Guest Houses In Britain

A guest hotel or guest house is a vacation hotel where guests generally
stay for several days or up to a couple of weeks. Usually meals are included in
the price. Guests take walks around the area, engage in sports such as fishing
or golf and drive to points of interest. Often these places have recreational
facilities on the property. Sometimes the management provides a program - -
morning or evening devotions at the table, slide shows at night, etc. - - sometimes not. Most if not all of these facilities are located in prime tourist areas
such as Britain's southwest coastal region or the Scottish islands. Some are
owned by missions organizations, others are private enterprises. All have links
with the evangelical community and draw Christian guests primarily if not
exclusively. In some places the same people return year after year. One is
bound to meet a cross section of British Christians at these places. They are
probably a better deal for couples or families than for young singles. A car is
almost a necessity in most places. Upon request, the management will send
their latest brochure with a full description, prices, etc. Advance booking is
recommended. For a more extensive coverage of vacation possibilities in
Britain from a Christian perspective there is a little paperback available in
England called the CHRISTIAN HOLIDAY GUIDE by Joan Bristow (price .95p).
This can be obtained in Christian bookstores in England or from Marshall,
Morgan and Scott Publishers, 116 Baker St., London W1M 2BB.

Arundel House, 12-13 Arundel Terrace, Brighton BN2 1GL   tel. 0273/64558
 Overlooks the sea front. Brighton is a popular weekend resort just an
 hour by train from London. The house is owned by the Baptist Union.

Belsfield Christian Hotel, Pentire Crescent, Newquay, Cornwall   tel. 3259
 Near the beach and a short walk from the center of town.

Burnside Hotel, West Moulin Road, Pitlochery PH16 5EA, Scotland tel. 0796.2203
 Pitlochery is one of the most popular highlands resorts.

Corestin Christian Guest House, Port Isaac, North Cornwall   tel. Port Isaac 267
 Not far from the legendary castle of King Arthur. Overlooks the sea.

The Croft Guest House, Lydiate Lane, Lynton, Devon EX35 6HE   tel. 2931
 Near the coast and the moors of the beautiful southwest county of Devon.

Christian Holiday Home, The Rookery, Lynton, Devon EX35 6LB
 On the North Devon coast near Exmoor National Park.

Craig-Ard Christian Guest House, Millport, Isle of Cumbrae, Scotland tel. 532
    An island in the Firth of Clyde on Scotland's west coast.

Dunringell Hotel, Kyleakin, Isle of Skye, Scotland   tel. Kyleakin 280
    Has its own $4\frac{1}{2}$ acre grounds on the outskirts of the village.

Emmaus Christian Guest House, West Parade, West Shore, Llandudno,
North Wales   tel. 77057
    A good center for sightseeing in North Wales.

Felmingham Hall, North Walsham, Norfolk   tel. Swanton Abbot 228
    An Elizabethan manor house dating to 1569 on 60 acres of parkland.

Greenfields, Field Road, Southerndown, nr. Bridgend,
Glam., South Wales   tel. 638
    On the popular South Wales coast.

Haldon Court, 34 Douglas Avenue, Exmouth, Devon EX8 2HB   tel. 3836
    Good family place close to sandy beaches.

Hamilton Arms, Shiskine, Isle of Arran, Scotland   tel. Shiskine 333
    Beautiful scenery, good center for hiking, golfing, pony riding, etc.

Hatfield Court, Leominster, Herefordshire   tel. Steen's Bridge 287
    Farm guest house in the west of England.

Hazel Dene, 24 Daventry Avenue, Bispham, Blackpool   tel. Blackpool 53926
    Small guest house near the Promenade in this popular seaside resort.

Hebron Brae, Lodgehill Road, Nairn, Scotland   tel. Nairn 3459
    Modern guest house on the Moray Firth near Inverness.

The Hollies, 7 Mornington Road, Southport, Lancs. PR9 OTS   tel. 55177
    Hotel in coastal resort not far from Liverpool and Manchester.

Holly Lane, Tansley, nr. Matlock, Derbys.   tel. Matlock 2100
    Country guest house in England's peak district.

Homelea, Chilsworthy, Holsworthy, Devon
    Guest house in a small village 2 miles from the market town of Holsworthy.
    Board only on weekends. Good center for touring Devon and Cornwall.

Ingleside Hotel, Lynton, Devon   tel. 059/85 2223
    Small country hotel not far from many places of scenic beauty.

Lakeview Guest House, Drumcrow, Blaney, Enniskillen, Co. Fermanagh, North Ireland   tel. Derrygonnelly 263
  Guest house on a 40 acre farm overlooking Lower Lough Erne. Good walking center.

Ledard, 94 Brisbane Road, Largs, Ayrshire, Scotland   tel. Largs 3272
  Guest house on the Ayrshire coast.

Lyndhurst Christian Hotel, 4 Park Terrace, Bognor Regis, Sussex tel. 23254
  On the seafront in a select part of town.

Lynwood Christian Guest House, 11a Leicester St., Southport, Lancs. PR9 0ER
  Near the Promenade in a popular seaside resort.

Maranatha Christian Hotel, Lower Torrs Park, Ilfracombe, North Devon tel. Ilfracombe 3245
  Near the sea front. A good center for coastal walks and sea trips.

Marlborough Christian Hotel, 54 Kirkley Cliff, Lowestoft, Suffolk tel. 3750
  Located in sunny East Anglia on England's east coast.

The Meadows, Lowick Green, nr. Ulverston, Lancs. LA12 8DX tel. 276
  Good center for touring the Lake District. Hotel has its own grounds.

Merrymead Guest House, Cheese Lane, Sidmouth, Devon EX10 8RA
  On the south coast not far from Exeter and Dartmoor.

Montpelier Christian Guest House, Lladrindod Wells, Powys, Wales tel 2385
  The annual Keswick in Wales convention is held here the first week in August. A good center for touring Wales, and for walking.

Netherhall, Largs, Ayrshire, Scotland   tel. Largs 2084
  Guest house and conference center on spacious grounds on the Firth of Clyde. Some of Scotland's finest scenery is within easy reach of here.

Oak Hall, 9 Wilfred Road, Boscombe, Bournemouth tel. 0202/35062
  Private hotel on the south coast near beaches and the New Forest.

Orleans Christian Guest House, 8 Lathom Road, Southport, Lancs. PR9 0JA
  Near the Promenade, pier and other attractions of this seaside resort.

Overcliff Christian Guest House, 2 Trefusis Terrace, Exmouth, Devon EX8 2AX
  Within view of the coast and Exe estuary and near Exeter, Dartmoor and other places of interest on England's south coast.

Pamington Farm, Tewkesbury, Glous.   tel. Bredon 396
    Guest accommodations on a Cotswold farm. A good center for touring
    the west of England.

The Place Hotel, St. Columb Minor, Newquay, Cornwall tel. Newquar 5880
    The hotel stands in grounds of over 2 acres and is within walking distance
    of the beach. Conference center for the Movement for World Evangelization.

Salem Christian Guest House, St. Lawrence, Ventnor, Isle of Wight tel. 852838
    Stands in 3 acres of woodland and has a sea view.

Sidmount Hotel, Station Road, Sidmouth, Devon EX10 8XJ tel. Sidmouth 3432
    A half mile from the coast and within easy reach of many points of interest.

Spindrift House, Marazion, Cornwall   tel. Marazion 710298
    A 200 year old hotel with modern facilities not far from Land's End

Summerhill Christian Guest House, Culver Road, Shanklin, Isle of Wight
    Has its own grounds and is just 5 minutes away from the beach.

Towell Farm, Beaford, Winkleigh, North Devon tel. Beaford 210
    Country place providing room and breakfast only.

Tregonwell Guest House, Tors Road, Lynmouth, Devon tel. Lynton 3369
    Beside the River Lyn a few minutes walk from the beach. A good center
    for walking, fishing and touring Exmoor National Park.

Welsbeare, Poughill, Crediton, Devon tel. Cheriton Fitzpaine 395
    A guest house in the beautiful mid-Devon countryside.

Wingate Farm, Countisbury, Lynton, Devon   tel. Brendon 285
    On the North Devon coast. A good place for walks on the cliffs and moors,
    and for touring scenic spots in Somerset and Devon.

Zion House, 120 Melmount Road, Strabane, Co. Tyrone, North Ireland
    Guest house and conference center in scenic countryside. Fishing, golf
    and many other types of recreation available. A good center for touring
    Northern Ireland by car.

b. The VCH Hotels In Europe

There are over 250 VCH (Verband Christlicher Hospize or Association of Christian Private Hotels) in Europe, mainly in the Germanys, Scandinavia and Switzerland, but including a few in Austria, France, Italy, Belgium and England. These hotels range in price and accommodations from modest pensions and missions-hotels to quite luxurious first and second class establishments. They are united by a commitment to the Christian faith which is reflected in their attitude toward their guests. Unlike the English guest houses, however, most cater to the general public, though there are certain to be Christian people staying there at any given time. They may or may not provide a Christian program, but will be glad to arrange meeting space for groups. New descriptive brochures are issued each year with up-to-date prices, etc. These will give the complete list of VCH hotels in W. Germany, the DDR, Denmark, Norway, Sweden or Switzerland, and will include the list of hotels in other countries. Obtain these from the following:

Verband Christlicher Hospize,
6200 Wiesbaden,
Schutzenhofstr. 9,
 W. Germany

Verband Christlicher Hospize,
X-104 Berlin,
Albrechtstr. 8,
 German Democratic Republic

Denmark Missions-Hotels,
Longangstraede 27,
DK-Copenhagen,
 Denmark

Norwegian Missions-Hotels,
Forbundshotellet,
Holbergsplass 1,
N-Oslo,
 Norway

Swedish Christian Hotels,
Elsa Brandstroms,
Gata 3, 3 tr,
S-58227 Linkoping,
 Sweden

Swiss Verband Christlicher Hospize,
Hotel-Pension de Famille,
CH-1800 Vevey,
  Switzerland

The addresses given below are some of the VCH hotels in main centers.
It is complete only in the case of Belgium, France, Italy and England:

AUSTRIA
CVJM-Hospiz-Hotel,   (room and breakfast only)
Kenyonsgasse 15,
A-1070 Vienna VII   tel. (0043) 222/93 13 04

Schweizerhaus-Salzburg,   (room and breakfast or full board)
Raphael-Donner-Str. 25,
A-5026 Salzburg-Aigen   tel. (0043)62 22/2 34 43

BELGIUM
Centre Evangélique,   (large old building with grounds - good for a group)
5531-Flavion   tel. (082) 68 83 01

DENMARK
Missionshotellet,
Longangstraede 27,
1468 Copenhagen   tel. (01) 12 65 70

Missionshotellets Annex
Vester Voldgade 89,
1552 Copenhagen   tel. (01) 11 48 06

Missionshotellet "Hebron",
Helgolandsgade 4,
1653 Copenhagen   tel. (01) 31 69 06

Missionshotellet "Ansgar",
Colbjornsensgade 29,
1653 Copenhagen   tel. (01) 21 21 96

Missionshotellet "Nebo",
Istedage 6,
1650 Copenhagen   tel. (01) 21 12 17

(The missions-hotels are associated with the Lutheran Church in the Scandinavian countries. They are generally well run, comfortable but not luxurious, and moderate in price. Some have cafeterias or restaurants with good meals, also at attractive prices. Most missions-hotels hold optional Christian services a few times each week.)

ENGLAND
    CVJM-Hospice   (Just south of Paddington Station near Hyde Park)
    Lancaster Hall Hotel,
    Craven Terrace,
    London, W. 2   tel. 723-9276

ITALY
    Casa della Diaconesse Germaniche di Kaiserswerth,   (Guesthouse)
    Via Allesandro Farnese 18,
    00192 Rome   tel. 35 25 61

NORWAY
    Ansgar Misjonshotell,   (See note on Denmark)
    Mollergt. 26,
    Oslo 1   tel. 20 47 35

    Filadelfia Hotell og Kafé,
    St. Olavs gt. 24,
    Oslo 1   tel. 20 00 15

    Stefanhotellet,
    Rosenkrantz gt. 1,
    Oslo 1   tel. 33 62 90

    Grand Hotell Terminus,
    Kong Oscars gt. 71,
    5000 Bergen   tel. 21 66 55

    Bibelskolens Sommerhotell,
    C. Sundtsgt. 22,
    5000 Bergen   tel. 21 25 31

    Trondelag Misjonshotell,
    Kongens gt. 26,
    7000 Trondheim   tel. 2 83 48

    Norrona Misjonshospits A/S,
    Thomas Angels gt. 20,
    7000 Trondheim   tel. 2 00 14

FRANCE
    Hotel Savournin,   (Between Nice and Cannes on the
    15, Avenue Auguste Renoir,   French Riviera)
    Cagnes sur Mer   Tel. 20 60 58

    Hotel Pax,   (Restaurant in hotel. Located
    24, rue du faubourg National,   close to the train station.)
    Strasbourg   tel. (88) 32 14 54

GERMANY, West
    Puckler-Hospiz,   (In central area)
    Schonwalder Strasse 21,
    1 Berlin 65   tel. (030) 461-8060

    Hotel Frankfurter Hospiz,
    Eckenheimer Landstr. 178,
    6 Frankfurt/Main   tel. (o611) 55 01 55

    CVJM Gaste-Service GmbH,   (Close to the main train station)
    Landwehrstrasse 13,
    8 Munich 2   tel. (089) 55 59 41

    Hotel Wartburg-Hospiz,   (Restaurant in hotel)
    Lange Str. 49,
    7 Stuttgart   tel. (0711) 22 19 91   (Air conditioned restaurant.)

GERMANY, East (Deutsche Demokratische Republik)
    Hospiz am Bahnhof Friedrichstrasse,   (Restaurant in hotel)
    Albrechtstrasse 8,
    X-104 Berlin   tel. 422-5696

    Christliches Hospiz,   (Central area near Marx-Engles-Platz)
    Auguststrasse 82,
    X-104 Berlin   tel. 422-5321

    Christliches Hospiz,   (Restaurant in hotel)
    Ross Strasse 14,
    X-701 Leipzig   tel. 2 62 12

SWEDEN

Hotel Excelsior,
Birger Jarlsgatan 35,
Stockholm   tel. (08) 22 07 20

Hotell Tegnérlunden,
Tegnérgat. 8,
Stockholm   tel. (08) 34 97 80

Hotell Ansgar,
Bryggargat. 10,
Stockholm   tel. (08) 23 04 70

Fralsningsarméns hotell Ritz,
Burggrevegat. 25, (Post Box 484)
401 27 Goteborg 1   tel. (031) 17 52 60

SWITZERLAND

Hotel Kreuz,
Zeughausgasse 41,
BE 3001 Bern   tel. 22 11 62

(Hotel standards in Switzerland
 are among the finest in the world,
 and the Christian hotels are no
 exception)

Hotel de l'Ancre,
rue de Lausanne 34,
GE 1200 Geneva   tel. 22 377

Ferienheim Abendruh,
BE 3800 Interlaken   tel. 22 69 16

Hotel Johanniterhof,
Nahe Bahnhof,
LU 6002 Lucerne   tel. 23 18 55

Hotel Garni Seilerhof,
Haringstr. 20,
ZH 8000 Zurich tel. 32 07 84

Hotel Garni Bristol,
Stampfenbachstr. 34,
ZU 8000 Zurich   tel. 47 07 00

c. Swiss Church Hostels

There are throughout Switzerland many church related hostels or retreat centers, all of which are open to the Christian public (and in some cases to the general public). These places are especially suitable for groups, but most take individual guests. All serve meals. Organizations can send for a descriptive booklet (in German) listing details on all the facilities to

The Swiss Institute of Pastoral Sociology, Post fach 909, CH-9001 St. Gallen Ask for information on church institutional houses in Switzerland (Kirchliche Bildungshauser). Individuals can send to any particular facility and ask for a descriptive brochure. Be sure to enclose a couple of international postal certificates to facilitate a quick reply. In general, prices are very reasonable at these places. Many are located in beautiful surroundings, and the accommodations (as in all of Switzerland) are sparkling clean and pleasant, though not luxurious. In most places there are no programs in the summer of a Christian nature, but groups are welcome to put on their own. Below is a complete listing of addresses with a few notes:

Le Cenacle, 17 Promenade Charles Martin, 1208 Geneva (all are in Switzerland) 022/ 36 47 93

Centre de Rencontres de Cartigny, 1236 Cartigny (For adults - a bit expensive, but beautiful) 022/56 12 10

La Coque, 1261 Trelex   022/69 13 06

Maison de Monteret, 1264 St.- Cergue   022/60 12 85

Foyer de Tours, 1562 Corcelles-Pres-Payerne   037/61 21 08

Villa Vandel, 1618 Chatel-Saint-Denis   021/56 71 25

Foyer de Retraite, 1661 Montbarry - Le Paquier   029/2 55 31

Couvent des Capucins, 1680 Romont   037/52 21 51

Bildungszentrum Burgbuhl, 1713 St. Antoni   037/35 11 73 (Catholic place. Good.)

Notre-Dame du Rosaire, 1772 Grolley   037/45 14 38

Foyer de Charite "Dents-du-Midi", 1880 Bex   025/5 22 22

Notre-Dame du Silence, Chemin de la Sitterie 2, 1950 Sion   027/2 42 20

Camp de Vaumarcus, 2038 Vaumarcus   038/55 22 44 (Old place. Inexpensive)

Centre de Jeunesse et de Formation "Le Louverain", 2206 Les Geneveys-Sur-
     Coffrane   038/57 16 66   (Modern facility. Recommended)

Centre de Sornetan, 2711 Sornetan   032/91 95 35   (Modern place. Good)

Centre St. Francois/Bildungszentrum Montcroix, Chemin du Vorbourg,
     2800 Delemont   066/22 39 55
Reformierte Heimstatte, 3645 Gwatt   033/36 31 31 (Largest Christian center in
     Switzerland. Fantastic lakeside setting. Recommended.)
Jugendhaus und Heimstatte "Alpina" der Evangelisch-Methodistischen Kirche,
     3715 Adelboden   033/73 22 25 (Methodist church center in mountainous
     setting. Recommended.)
St. Jodernheim, 3930 Visp   028/6 22 69

Evangelische Heimstatte der Nordwestschweiz Leuenberg, 4434 Holstein Bl
     061/97 14 81   (Modern facility. Good)
Franziskushaus Dulliken, 4657 Dulliken   062/22 20 22

Tagungszentrum Reformierte Heimstatte auf dem Rugel, 5707 Seegen
     064/54 16 03   (Lakeside setting. Very nice)
Haus Bruchmatt, Bruchmattstrasse 9, 6003 Lucerne   041/22 40 33
     (Located in the center of Lucerne)
Seminar St. Beat, Adlingenswilerstrasse 15, 6006 Lucerne   041/23 65 22

Haus Bethanien, 6066 St. Niklausen   041/66 53 66

Aufgebothaus, 6073 Flueli   041/66 55 66

Ferien/und Schulungszentrum Viktoria, 6082 Reuti-Hasliberg   036/71 11 21
     (Fine view of the mountains. Good)
Bildungs/und Ferienzentrum Matt, 6103 Schwarzenberg   041/97 28 35

Bad Schonbrunn, 6311 Edlibach   042/52 16 44

Heimstatte SPM (Schweizerische Pfingstmission), 6376 Emmetten 041/64 25 55
     (Pentecostal center. New place in the Alps. Good)
Antoniushaus Mattli, 6443 Morschach   043/31 22 26 (Modern center near
     Lake Lucerne. Good)
Campo Enrico Pestalozzi, 6611 Arcegno   093/35 14 87 (Located in Italian
     Switzerland. Simple, inexpensive accommodations)

Casa S. Pio X, Via Nassa 64, 6900 Lugano   091/3 21 34 (Italian Switzerland)

Convento Santa Maria, 6951 Bigorio   091/91 12 22   (Italian Switzerland)

Evangelisches Zentrum fur Ferien und Bildung, 6983 Magliaso   091/71 14 41
    (Very good. In Italian part)
Randolins, Evangelisches Zentrum fur Ferien und Bildung, 7500 St. Moritz
    082/3 43 05   (In Switzerland's most popular ski resort)
Paulusakademie, Carl-Spittelerstrasse 38, Postfach 361, 8053 Zurich
    01/53 34 00Schaffhauser Reformierte Heimstatte, 8455 Rudlingen
Schaffhauser Reformierte Heimstatte, 8455 Rudlingen   01/96 62 98
    (Near the Rhine River and Rhine Falls. Good place)
Haus Neukirch, 8578 Neukirch an der Thur   072/3 14 35

Tagungs/und Studienzentrum Boldern, 8708 Mannedorf   01/922 11 71
    (Above the lake near Zurich. Recommended)
Schweizer Jugend/und Bildungszentrum, 8840 Einsiedeln   055/53 42 95

Evangelische Heimstatte Bienenheim, 8873 Amden   058/46 12 26

Neu-Schonstatt, 8883 Quarten   085/4 11 61

Alemannenhaus, 8890 Flums   085/3 28 15

Seminar St. Georgen, 9011 St. Gallen   071/22 74 30

Heimstatte Schloss Wartensee, Ostschweizerisches Evangelisches
    Tagungszentrum, 9400 Rorschacherberg   071/41 16 26   (An old castle
    above a lake. Good)
Galluszentrum Wildhaus - Lisighaus, 9658 Wildhaus   074/5 12 43

d. Miscellany of Other Christian Places To Stay

As the title suggests, this section will deal with various other Christian places to stay in Europe, and also a bit of information about two types of non-religious accommodations that are inexpensive and present an opportunity to meet fellow travelers.

AMSTERDAM CHRISTIAN YOUTH HOSTELS

There are two Christian hostels in Amsterdam, both in the central area. Their purpose is partly evangelistic, as they cater to the thousands of young people who stream through Amsterdam in search of fun, adventure and dope. However, they will also take Christian young people, individually or in groups, depending upon available space. It is a wise idea to write ahead and not to depend upon the chance of finding a bed at the last minute. They are:

Eben Haezer, Bloemstraat 179   tel. 24 47 17

The Shelter, Barndesteeg 21   tel. 25 32 30

THE TORCHBEARER CENTERS

The Capernwray Fellowship of Torchbearers (covered in B.1 under Bible Schools) also opens some of their centers to Christian groups during the summer months. Generally, the center provides a conference type program with meetings morning and evening and various recreation possibilities, and a group coming in can fit in with this and arrange some of their own activities as well. The centers are located in beautiful parts of the country, so that hiking, swimming, mountain climbing, etc., are especially attractive. Staying for a week or two at one of these places also provides an American group with the opportunity to meet some European Christian young people. Meetings are often conducted in English, or translation is arranged. For further information, group organizers should write directly to the centers. Advance booking is a necessity, as these accommodations often fill up several months to a year ahead of time. Prices are moderate - - in the area of $5.00 to $7.00 a day per person, full board. Like all prices in Europe, they are rising each year, of course, so ask for exact quotes:

Schloss Klaus, Mr. Peter Wiegand, Director   (See Historio-Guide
A-4564 Klaus /Steyr,   for Austria)
Oberosterreich, Austria

Tauernhof, Mr. Gernot Kunzelmann, Director
A-8970 Schladming,
Coburgstrasse 50,
Styr, Austria

Bodenseehof, Rev. Charles E. Moore, Director
D-799 Friedrichshafen 2,
Ziegeistrasse 15,
Germany

Klostermuehle, Mr. Bernhard Rebsch, Director
D-5409 Obernhof/Lahn,
Germany

Holsby Brunn, Rev. Fred Wright, Director
570 15 Holsbybrunn,
Sweden

Mar Cristalino, Mr. Reimer Nae
Archiduque Carlos 70-26A,
Valencia 14,
Spain

BIBLE SCHOOLS

Many of the Bible schools in Britain and Continental Europe will accommodate Christian parties or even small groups during the summer, and in many
cases can provide meals as well as beds. See section B.1 for complete listing of
names and addresses. The usual rule applies - - inquire in advance. Because
these accommodations are such a good deal they are often taken even years
ahead of time. But, again, they do have cancellations and some space available
from time to time, so it is worth checking into if you are planning a group tour.

SCHLOSS MITTERSILL AND CASA MOSCIA

Schloss Mittersill and Casa Moscia are Christian student conference
centers located in Austria and Switzerland. The movements owning them (the
International Fellowship of Evangelical Students and the Swiss VBG) do not use
them all year round, and therefore are glad to rent space to other Christian
organizations when it is available.

Schloss Mittersill was once a Medieval castle, the seat of the Bishop of
Salzburg, and more recently it was an exclusive hunting club catering to
movie stars and some of the crowned heads of Europe. Now it has been
completely remodeled as a conference center, including pleasant dormitory
rooms, a meeting room equipped with the latest translation hardware and a
fantastic restaurant sized kitchen. One part of the castle has been kept as a

hotel, however, and is rented out to couples, families or individuals on a nightly or weekly basis. Mittersill is in the Pinzgau Valley just west of Zell-am-See in the heart of the Austrian Alps. It is on the main highway from Munich to Venice (by way of the Felber Tunnel). Schloss Mittersill can handle groups of around 60 people in the student section. For full information and latest prices, write to the manager, Mr. Wolfgang Fry, Schloss Mittersill, A-5730 Mittersill, Land Salzburg, Austria.

Casa Moscia is a villa on the shore of Lake Maggiore just outside the Italian-Swiss town of Ascona. Accommodations here are more limited, but they can take 25 people or so. The main attraction is the dream-like lake, dotted with little islands and surrounded by dramatic mountains. In the summer the swimming and boating are excellent, with facilities at Moscia for both. Nearby Locarno is an interesting place to visit, and Milan is an easy day trip by car. For more information, write to Mr. Franz Luthy, Director, Casa Moscia International Student Centre, 6612 Ascona, Switzerland.

Both Mittersill and Moscia are off the main train routes. A narrow guage railroad goes from Zell-am-See to Krimmel by way of Mittersill, but the nearest train station to Moscia is at Locarno.

CHRISTIAN HOSTELS AND GUEST HOUSES IN ITALY

These places are run by churches or Christian organizations, and their purpose is to accommodate Christian travelers, or sometimes just travelers in general, who don't have a lot of money to spend. Some welcome groups.

Hotel YMCA
Piazza Independenza 23/c,
00185 Rome   tel. 06/46 49 21

(This place is advertised as a 2nd class hotel, and thus is an exception to the above description. It would, however, still be a good value.)

Foresteria Valdese
Palazzo Cavagnis,
Calle Lunga, S. Maria Formosa,
30122 Venice

(A nice place in the central area run by the Waldensians - above their church, as a matter of fact. They will take individuals, families or groups.)

Foresteria "Concordia"
Via Casa di Majo, 28 bis,
80075 Forio d'Ischia (NA) tel. 89 73 24

(A guest house on the Island of Ischia near Naples run by the Salvation Army)

The Servicemen's Center
Piazzetta Matilde Serao, 7,
Naples   tel. 39 87 45

(Primarily for service personnel, but Christian young people are welcome. No rooms, but there are free meals and a program each evening. Run by the Conservative Baptists.)

Casa Valdese per Ferie (or Waldensian Vacation House)
Piazza Mazzini, 1,
57038 Rio Marina (LI)   Island of Elba

(Open to Protestants of all denominations)

Albergo Svizzero "La Vela"   (Run by the Swiss Reformed Church.
Via Vittorio Veneto 35,   Located near Savona on the Italian Riviera.
17022 Borgo Verezzi (SV)   tel. 6 80 03   For conferences and adult groups.)

Foresteria dell 'Esercizio della Salvezza (Salvation Army)
Via Aretina 91,   (A very nice place, but only 12 beds)
50136 Florence   tel. 67 24 45

Istituto Gould, Marco Jourdan, Director   (A Christian guest house, which
Via dei Serragli, 49,   tends to be very busy during the summer)
50124 Florence tel. 055/57 25 76

Ostello Santa Monaca   (A youth hostel run by the Catholics.
Via Santa Monaca,   Centrally located, and no membership
50124 Florence   needed. Clean, cheap and plenty of hot
                                            showers. Youth hostel rules apply.)

NOT CHRISTIAN - - BUT GOOD AND INEXPENSIVE

Two types of accommodation that offer low cost and interesting possibilities
for meeting other travelers are the youth hostels and university dormitories.
Youth hostels, of course, are open primarily to young people and have various
rules and restrictions necessary to keep them running efficiently. They vary in
quality, being generally cleaner and more pleasant in Germany, Switzerland and
Scandinavia than in the southern countries. However, for the money it is difficult
to do much better. For general information, write to The American Youth Hostels
Hostels, Inc., Delaplane, VA 22025. Essentials are the membership card and
the YHA International Handbook, vol. 1 <u>Europe.</u>

University dorms are open throughout Britain during the summer. Generally
the rooms are twins, though it is possible to get a single bed or a room with
three or four beds. Some of the universities are very beautiful and romantic
places - - the halls of ivy and all that - - and the price is right. Often meals
can be arranged, breakfast at least. Parking is easier than in down town areas.
For a complete listing, write to University Holidays, Ltd., Borehamgate House,
Sudbury, Suffolk CO10 6ED, England. Students can request a booklet from the
British Travel Authority, 680 5th Ave., New York, NY 10019, called "British
Youth Accommodations. "

5. Christian Conventions, Conferences and Communities

Visitors from North America are welcome at several annual conventions held in Britain, and at various conference and retreat centers and evangelical communities both in Britain and Continental Europe. Some of the annual gatherings are gigantic, involving many thousands of people. All of the events and places afford the opportunity for contact with fellow Christians of a different cultural background and for participation in meaningful spiritual exercises and activities. The British conferences have the obvious advantage of being held in English, whereas a knowledge of another European language, particularly German, may be necessary at some of the European centers. However, the listings in this book are primarily of international meetings and places, and for obvious reasons no attempt has been made to include all of the Christian conferences held annually in Europe, or all of the various spiritual communities. As in the case of most all the information included in EUROPE ON PURPOSE, there is always the necessity of confirmation. Those interested are urged to write directly for the latest schedules, prices and requirements for attendance. Ask for specific information on housing. Don't forget to enclose the usual international postal certificates for a quick reply.

a. British Conventions

The Bangor Worldwide Missionary Convention
This is the largest missionary convention held in the British Isles. It takes
place the last week in August in the historic North Ireland city of Bangor.
For information, write to the Secretary, Mr. Raymond Pitt, 15 Ranfurly
Avenue, Bangor, Co. Down, North Ireland (tel. 60868)

General Conference of the Assemblies of God
Up to 8000 people attend this great annual conference held in May. For
information write to The Assemblies of God in Great Britain and Ireland,
106-114 Talbot Street, Nottingham NG1 5GH, England

The Fountain Trust Conferences
The Fountain Trust, an organization interested in church renewal and in
the gifts of the Holy Spirit, sponsors several conferences in Britain each
year. One such, featuring speakers such as Cardinal Leon Joseph Suenens
and Agnes Sanford, will be held on August 1-5, 1977, at Central Hall,
Westminster (London). For details, write to The Fountain Trust,
23 Spencer Road, East Molesey, Surrey KT8 OSP, England (tel. 979-1798)

The Movement For World Evangelization Conference (Filey Conference)
This conference (or Holiday Crusade) for the deepening of the Christian
experience is held each year in September at Filey on England's Yorkshire
coast. The conference takes over an entire 500 acre camp, and draws
thousands of Christians. For information on the Crusade or other activities
of this organization, write to The Movement For World Evangelization,
10 Cuthbert Road, Croydon, Surrey CRO 3RB, England

The Keswick Convention
The Keswick Convention, a conference for the deepening of the spiritual
life, was first held in this picturesque Lakeland village over 100 years ago,
and "Keswick" has become a household word among evangelical Christians
around the world. Some six thousand or more people attend the convention,
which occurs in July (in recent years there have been two conferences,
running a week each, with an emphasis on families the second week).
Information may be obtained from The Secretary, The Keswick Convention,
231 Merseside Way North, Solihull, Warwickshire, West Midlands B92 7AY,
England

Keswick In Wales and The Greystones Keswick
 Smaller "Keswicks" are held each year in Wales (first week in August) and
 in Ireland (first week in July). For details, write to the following:
 "Keswick-In Wales," Montpelier Christian Guest House,
 Llandrindod Wells, Powys, Mid-Wales   (Tel. 2385)

 "Greystones Keswick," Carrig Eden,
 Marine Road, Greystones, Co. Wicklow, Republic of Ireland

The Unevangelized Fields Mission Holiday Convention
 An annual Bible Missionary Convention is held each year by this missionary
 organization. For details, write to The Unevangelized Fields Mission,
 9 Gunnersbury Avenue, London W5 3NL, England

b. Conference Centers In Britain

 In contrast to the annual conventions, which in most cases are held for a
week or two once a year, the conference centers have facilities which can be
rented by Christians almost any time during the year. Often they are located in
very interesting and beautiful parts of the country. In many cases they are open
for booking by individuals as well as by groups. Most have programs that guests
can plug into. However, it is possible for parties to set up their own programs,
and for individuals to just have a quiet retreat without going to a lot of meetings.
Blaithwaite House, Wigton, Cumbria CA7 OAZ, England   tel. Wigton 2319
 Old house set in 250 acres of farm and woodland near the Lake District.
Cliff Conference Centre, Calver, via Sheffield, S30 1XG   tel. Baslow 2321/2
 On the grounds of Cliff College in the Derbyshire Peak District.
Cloverley Hall, Whitchurch, Shropshire SY13 4PH   tel. Calverhall 217
 A conference center owned by the Irish Gospel Outreach. Good location for
 touring the west of England and Wales.
Herne Bay Court Evangelical Centre, Ltd., Canterbury Road, Herne Bay,
Kent CT6 5TD   tel. 0227-3 3254
 Holiday and conference place situated in secluded grounds near the sea.
Kilcreggan House, Argyll Road, Kilcreggan, Dumbartonshire G84 OTJ,
Scotland   tel. Kilcreggan 2318
 Holiday and missionary conference center run by the Worldwide
 Evangelization Crusade (WEC). Large house in five acres of woodland
 close to Loch Lomond and other famous Scottish beauty spots.

Kilravock Christian Centre, Croy, Inverness IVl 2PJ, Scotland Tel. Croy 258
This is the 15th century Kilravock Castle, home of Miss Elizabeth Rose, 25th chieftan of Clan Rose. Facilities include a guest house, a youth center and a conference hall seating 200. Accommodations for individuals, families (in the castle) or for groups (in the dorms).

Lee Abbey, Lynton, North Devon EX35 6JJ tel. Lynton 2303
A large country house in the North Devon coastland run by a community of Christian men and women. Short conferences (houseparties) are offered regularly.

Scargill House, Kettlewell, Skipton, Yorkshire BD23 5HU tel. Kettlewell 234
A place for small conferences and private guests run by a Christian community of lay people related to the Anglican Church. The community puts on a regular program of Bible studies, special speakers, etc. A good area for hiking, potholing, rock climbing.

St. Ninian's, Comrie Road, Crieff, Perthshire PH7 4BG tel. Crief 2484
This is a Christian training center run by the Church of Scotland. Groups or individual guests are welcome, and may join in with the training program or carry on their own activities. The training is evangelical and well recommended. The location makes it a good place from which to tour Scotland.

Walmer House Holiday Centre, 6 Ash Hill Road, Torquay, Devon tel. 22734
Good location in the south coastal area. Open to groups, families or individuals.

Woodlands, Brunel Manor, Watcombe Park, Torquay TQl 4SF tel. 37421
This is a large country manor standing in 10 acres of woodland close to the south coast. It is run by an independent Trust and open to Christian groups.

c. European Conferences and Communities

L'Abri
L'Abri is very well known among American evangelicals because of the books (and more lately the film and lecture series) of Dr. Francis Schaeffer. His wife, Edith Schaeffer, has also published a couple of very successful books, one telling the story of their work which is simply called L'ABRI. L'Abri is a Christian community housed in a group of chalets near the Alpine village of Huemoz (the nearest railroad station is at Ollon). All sorts of things happen

there - - concentrated study of Christianity and culture with extensive use of Dr. Schaeffer's tapes, lectures and discussions sometimes led by Dr. Schaeffer, sometimes by a member of his family or by a visiting lecturer such as art professor Dr. Hans Rookmaaker, etc. Occasionally there are concerts or other arty type activities. The L'Abri people try to make visitors welcome, but the popularity of the place sometimes makes this difficult. If you wish to visit or to study at L'Abri, the wise thing to do is to write and ask if there is space available. The address is
The L'Abri Fellowship, Chalet les Melezes, 1861 Huemoz sur Ollon, Switzerland

Canaan
   Canaan is a Christian community and retreat center near Darmstadt, Germany. It is run by the Evangelical Sisterhood of Mary, headed by Mother Basilea Schlink and Mother Martyria, who founded the movement in 1947 just after World War II (see the Historio-Guide). There are some similarities between Canaan and L'Abri in that both have been made famous by the writings of the founder. Mother Basilea has over 100 titles in print, and her works have been translated into more than 30 languages. The movement also puts a distinctive historical marker, white on black, on sites of Christian interest in Europe and throughout the Holy Land. Visitors from around the world visit Canaan. Some conferences during the year are held in English. For information, write to The Evangelical Sisterhood of Mary, 61 Darmstadt-Eberstadt,
   Heidelberger Landstrasse 107, postfach 29, Germany tel. 06161/51031

Mittersill
   Schloss Mittersill, the IFES castle in Austria (see section 4.d, hotels, etc.) also offers some conferences that are open to the Christian public, and which are held in English. At Christmas time there is a Holiday Ski Conference that is evangelistic in nature (Christian young people in Europe are invited to bring their non-Christian friends). There are also some Bible seminars held in the spring. For details of current programs, write to the manager,
Mr. Wolfgang Fry, Schloss Mittersill, A-5730 Mittersill, Land Salzburg, Austria

Other Evangelical Communities
   Three other evangelical communities, which are German speaking, are:
The Brotherhood of Christ, Selbitz, Germany

The Christ Bearers, Auerbach, Germany

The Liebenzell Mission, Bad Liebenzell, Germany

Ecumenical Communities
    71460 Taizé-Community, France
    This is perhaps the most popular spiritual community in Europe, drawing upwards of 18,000 people on special occasions. It is a Protestant monastery, with the purpose of the reconciliation of separated Christians and all people who are at enmity with one another.

    The Iona Abbey, Island of Iona, Scotland
    The Iona Community was started in the 1930's by Dr. George F. MacLeod, who resigned his parish to head up the rebuilding of the 6th century abbey. Iona attracts a large number of visitors each year, who attend services in the Abbey church. The members of the community itself work among deprived people in the Glasgow slums.

Bibliography
    Mellis, Charles J. COMMITTED COMMUNITIES 1977, Wm. Carey Library 3.95 This brand new book by the former head of the Missionary Aviation Fellowship deals with the history of evangelical communities and their impact in the world today. Exciting reading.

    Bristow, Joan CHRISTIAN HOLIDAY GUIDE 1974, Marshall, Morgan and Scott 95p. Gives details on cenference centers, conventions and crusades, guest houses and every sort of evangelical event and accommodation in Britain.

    Bloesch, Donald G. WELLSPRINGS OF RENEWAL 1974, Eerdmans 3.25 A survey of Protestant monasteries and renewal communities in the U.S. and Europe. Good description, some photos.

6. Evangelical Churches In Britain and Europe

Attending church in Europe is one way to make contact with the evangelical Christian community. It is also a good thing for a Christian traveler abroad to break the pace of sightseeing, business, studies, etc., and to meet with a body of believers for worship. It is not difficult to find churches to attend in most places in Europe where there is preaching based on the Bible. Furthermore, there are in most major cities Anglican churches and in some cases Baptist churches where services are held in English. The plan of this chapter is to give addresses of church head offices or sources where lists of local congregations may be obtained, followed by a selected list of English speaking, evangelical churches in main cities.

Please keep in mind that the church situation in Europe, particularly on the Continent, differs considerably from that in the United States and English speaking Canada. For sources of information about the present state of Christianity in Europe, see section II. C, The Christian Missionary In Europe. Very generally, churches in Europe tend to lack what we have come to call "body life," and the professional clergy carry on the main functions. Often there is a mixture of the Biblical and traditional, and a lack of sense of mission to the community. Much of the Bible teaching, evangelism and live fellowship that exists in Europe (though by no means all) takes place outside of the church organization through various movements that have come into being since World War II.

The following publish directories of local congregations:
The Commonwealth and Continental Church Society, 175 Tower Bridge Road, London SE1 2AQ, England   tel. 407-4588

> Send three international postal certificates for a directory of English speaking churches in Europe (West and East), the Middle East and Africa. The directory indicates whether a church is served by the CCCS (meaning that the minister or chaplain would be evangelical), and gives the denomination if other than Anglican. In many cases the minister's or chaplain's phone number is listed, and travelers are urged to seek help from this source if they are sick or in trouble. An invaluable book.

The Baptist World Alliance, 1628 16th St. NW, Washington, D.C. 20009

> Send for a brochure entitled "Baptists in Europe and the Near East: A Guide For Tourists . . ." Free, but send a 13¢ stamp to cover postage. A larger booklet called "Where Is the Baptist Church?" listing all European national

Baptist headquarters, local churches, holiday camps, theological semi-
naries, etc., may also be available from this address. Otherwise, request
from the Baptist World Alliance, European Office, 4 Southampton Row,
London WClB 4AB, England, and send four international postal certificates.

For a directory of Christian brethren assemblies in Britain and Europe, send
$3.25 to Everyday Publications, 230 Glebemount Avenue, Toronto, Ontario
M4C 3T4, Canada. Ask for "A List of Assemblies in Britain and Other
Parts." Postpaid.

The Evangelical Alliances are clearing houses for church and missions
information in a number of European countries. Their services are for
nationals and missionaries, primarily. If for some reason you are planning to
become involved in the Christian community in any part of Europe, then you
may need to know who represents the Evangelical Alliance in that particular
country. This information may be obtained from
The European Evangelical Alliance, Peter Schneider, Secretary,
D-1000 Berlin 41, Albestrasse 4, Germany   tel. 030/852 5029

Another source of missions information within Europe is an organization
which sponsored an Urbana-like missionary conference in 1975 at Lausanne,
and now has an office there. It is
The European Missionary Association (TEMA)
route d'Echallens 34, 1032 Romanel-sur-Lausanne, Switzerland
tel. 021/ 35 28 44

Here are headquarters of other large denominations:
Methodist Press and Information Service, Central Buildings, Westminster
SWlH 9NH, England

The World Methodist Council, 150 Route de Ferney, 1211 Geneva 20, Switzerland

The United Reformed Church, 86.Tavistock Place, London WClH 9RT, England

The Assemblies of God in Great Britain and Ireland, 106-114 Talbot Street,
Nottingham NGl 5GH, England

SELECTED LIST OF CHURCHES IN BRITAIN AND IRELAND

London, England
All Souls Church, Langham Place (near Oxford Circus) Rev. Michael
Baughen, vicar. tel. 580-6029. One of the most influential churches in
Europe with a live ministry in the center of tourist London. The former
vicar, the Rev. John Stott, now has a worldwide reputation.

St. Helen's, Bishopsgate   Rev. Dick Lucas, vicar. (Liverpool St. underground station, walk right) Another of London's great city churches. Historic building.

Duke Street Baptist Church, Richmond   Pastor William Freal. An internationally known church.

Westminster Chapel, Buckingham Gate (St. James Park underground station, turn left and walk a short block) Well known independent church associated with the former minister, Dr. Martin Lloyd Jones. Central London.

Lewin Road Baptist Church (charismatic), Streatha SW16   Rev. Douglas McBain, pastor.

Cholmeley Evangelical Church (brethren assembly), 272 Archway Road, Highgate N6 (Highgate underground station, walk south) Mr. Harold Davey, Secretary.

Edinburgh, Scotland
   Holy Rood Church (Church of Scotland), London Road, Abbey Hill
   Rev. James Phillips (From Princes Street take buses 4, 15, 44, 45)

   Charlotte Chapel (Baptist), Rose Lane (on Charlotte Square off Princes St.)
   Rev. Derek Prime, pastor. Well known church associated with the former pastor, the Rev. Allen Redpath.

   St. Thomas's Church (Church of England), Corstorphine Rd. Rev. John Wesson, vicar.

   Bruntsfield Evangelical Church (brethren assembly), 7 Leamington Terrace, (From Princes St. take buses 11, 15, 16, 23) Mr. David Aird, Secretary

Dublin, Republic of Ireland
   St. Kevin's Church (Church of Ireland)

   Dublin Central Mission (Methodist Church)

   Adelaide Road Church (Presbyterian Church)

   Merrion Hall (brethren assembly)

   All of the above are evangelical churches within a mile of the center of Dublin.

Belfast, North Ireland
>   Great Victoria Street Baptist Church, Rev. Timothy G. Alford, pastor

>   May Street Presbyterian Church, Rev. William Boland, minister

>   Victoria Memorial Hall, May St. (brethren assembly meeting in a former cinema)

>   All of the above are evangelical churches in the city center.

SELECTED LIST OF CHURCHES IN CONTINENTAL EUROPE (English speaking unless otherwise indicated)

Amsterdam, the Netherlands
>   The English Reformed Church (Church of Scotland), The Begijnhof (off the Spui) (see the HISTORIO-GUIDE) Rev. C.R.M. Bell   tel. 72 22 21

>   Christ Church, Groenburgwal 42 Rev. B. Bradley   tel. 24 88 77

Athens, Greece
>   Trinity Baptist Church, 3 Aristotelous St.

>   Free Evangelical Church of Greece, 3 Alkiviadou St. (The services are in Greek, but these noble people are encouraged by visitors and welcome them heartily)

Berlin, German Democratic Republic
>   Gubener Strasse Baptist Church, Kadinerstrasse 20

Berlin, West Germany
>   St. George's Garrison Church (military, but civilians welcome), Preussen Allée (off Heerstrasse), Charlottenburg   tel. 309-4144 Services are taken by various chaplains.

>   Berlin Baptist Church, Rothenburstrasse 12A Pastor Luther Morphis tel. 030/738 068

Brussels, Belgium
>   International Baptist Church, 17 Rue Jacque Hoton tel. 771-9275 Rev. Charles Long tel. 354-6440

Copenhagen, Denmark
>   The Christian Fellowship (Kristent Faelleskap) A new, live group of believers. For information about services call Mr. Ole Madsen at 02/85 23 10.

Kristus-Kirken, Baggesensgade 7 (Baptist church, services in Danish)

The American Church, Gjorlingsvej 10 (suburb of Copenhagen) tel. 43 47 85
Services in English, but not necessarily evangelical.

Geneva, Switzerland
   The Calvin Auditoire (Church of Scotland), Place Taconnerie (see HISTORIO-
   GUIDE) Rev. John Hood   tel. 982 909

Helsinki, Finland
   The American Church (Lutheran), Pengerkatu 9 Rev. Kai Antturi

Lisbon, Portugal
   Third Baptist Church, Rua Filipe Folque (Services in Portuguese)

Madrid, Spain
   Immanuel Baptist Church, Calle de Hernandez de Tejada tel. 407-4347
   Pastor James Foster   tel. 200-0899

Oslo, Norway
   Tabernaklet, Hausmannsagaten 22 (Baptist church, services in Norwegian)

   St. Edmund, Mollergatt 30 Rev. B. Horlock tel. 56 38 90 (Anglican, not
   a member of the CCCS)

Paris, France
   St. Michaels Church, 5 rue d'Aguesseau (central area)
   Rev. E.M.T. McLellan   tel. 073-0900

   Christian brethren assembly, 56 Cours de Vincennes (metro Nation)
   Alain Choiquier, Secretary (Live group, visitors welcome. French speaking)

   Emmanuel Baptist Church, 86 Rue des Bons Raisins, 92-Rueil-Malmaison
   (suburb of Paris) Pastor Everett H. Croxton   tel. 970-1688

Prague, Czechoslovakia
   Sbor Bratrske Jednoty Baptistu (Baptist Church), Vinohradska 68 (Services
   in Czech)

Rome, Italy
   Rome Baptist Church, Piazza San Lorenzo in Lucina 35   tel. 679-5302
   Pastor William C. Ruchti tel. 32 15 25

   St. Andrews Church (Church of Scotland), 7 Via Venti Settembre
   Rev. A.J. McLean   tel. 47 16 27

Salzburg, Austria
Salzburg Baptist Church, Schumacher Strasse 18   Pastor Tom Cleary
tel. 87 69 72

Stockholm, Sweden
Philadelphia Church, Rorstrandgata 3 (Huge evangelical church with 6000
membership. Services are in Swedish but English speaking visitors welcome)

Immanuels Church (Another very large Bible teaching church)

Sts. Peter and Sigfrid, Strandvagen 76 Rev. D. I. Strangeways tel. 85 66 77
(Anglican church, not member of CCCS)

Norrmalmskyrkan, Norrtullsgaten 37 (Baptist Church. Services in Swedish)

Warsaw, Poland
Baptist Church, Walicow 25 m. 8 (Services are in Polish)

Zurich, Switzerland
Baptist Church, Gheistrasse 31, Ruschlikon-Zurich (suburb)

CHRISTIAN LITERATURE CRUSADE BOOKSTORES IN EUROPE
For a refreshing contact with Biblical Christianity in various cities in
Europe, plan to drop into the CLC bookstores in the following places. Your
visit will also be an encouragement to the staff, who are engaged in this work
as a missions outreach. Often the stores are sources of local information about
the evangelical Christian scene, and also stock maps and other sightseeing
supplies:

AUSTRIA
Christlicher Bucher Dienst, Sparberbachgasse 15, A-8010 GRATZ

FRANCE
"La Colline," 26160 La Begude de Mazenc, DROME
2, rue La Chalotais, 35100 - RENNES
1, rue de la Loi, 68000 - MULHOUSE
1, Rue Anatole-France, 3400-MONTPELLIER
14, rue Ferdinant-Malet, 07130-ST. PERAY
1, rue de la Fonderie, 31000-TOULOUSE

GERMANY
Christlicher Bucher-Kreuzzug, D-2 HAMBURG 50

GIBRALTER
   Good News Store, 15, Cornwall's Lane

ITALY
   Crociata del Libro Cristiano, Via Ricasoli 97r, 50122 FLORENCE
   Via 27 Luglio 122, 98100 MESSINA, Sicily
   Corse di Porta Romana 79, 20122 MILAN
   (Gia centro Biblico), Via Carriera Grande, 37, 80139 NAPOLI (Naples)
   Via Fabretti 35-37, 06100 PERUGIA
   Via Brunetto Latini, 16, 90141 PALERMO

NETHERLANDS
   Evangelische Lektuur Kruistocht, J.J. Cremerplain 2-4, AMSTERDAM 1013

ENGLAND
   2 Cathedral Place, LONDON EC4M 7EY
Other Christian bookstores in London are
   The Scripture Union Bookstore, Wigmore Street (near Oxford Street)
   Pickering & Inglis, Ludgate Hill (just west of St. Paul's Cathedral
CLC has bookstores in the following places in Britain: Birmingham, Canterbury, Chatham, Southampton, Ipswich, Alresford, Leicester, Newcastle-Upon-Tyne, Norwich, Sheffield, Swansea, and Aberdeen, Dundee, and Inverness in Scotland.

7. Special Information For Travelers To the East

Want to make a trip to Eastern Europe? There is no reason that you shouldn't, and (except for the borders) you'll probably find it a surprisingly friendly and unsinister place. Some of the cities have highly interesting historical monuments, many of them related to Christianity (see the HISTORIO-GUIDE), and the countryside is sometimes like stepping back into a pastoral scene in the Medieval world.

The big question we want to deal with here is, What about the Christians in East Europe? The answer is, Why not see for yourself? It's not q u i t e that simple, of course, but if you have the address of a church (and some are given in this book) or have a personal contact with Christians, your presence will be an encouragement. That is, it c a n be an encouragement. Many Christians in the West have swallowed a lot of nonsense about cloak and dagger heroics in East Europe and imagine themselves getting into the act. On the other hand, there a r e dangers, not so much for the visitors as for the East Europe believers themselves, when well meaning westerners fail to understand the realities of the situation.

To speak to this point, I have invited two men with vast experience in this area to write down some words of advice. Here they are:

ADVICE FOR CHRISTIAN TOURISTS TRAVELING TO EASTERN EUROPE

Check your motives for going. If it is for "adventure" or if you would like to be thought of as a hero when you return, then frankly it would be best NOT to visit the churches, and certainly not to try to visit any believers. The Communists are not playing games. They are deadly serious about their intentions to eradicate all forms of "religion," which in their view is "the opium of the people."

Be a good ambassador for Christ and your country. Be friendly. Have the attitude, "I'm here to learn about your country and customs because I'm interested in you." Take along a supply of ball-point pens and chewing gum - - these will come in handy when the language barrier becomes frustrating, and will usually be accepted gratefully.

If you are a dedicated follower of fashion, you'll stand out like a sore thumb in Eastern Europe. If you intend to visit churches and fellowship with the believers, dress modestly. And women please note: shorts, jeans and pant-suits are not acceptable in their culture.

Visit churches by all means - - and if you have a Bible with you in their language, leave it in the pew. Don't try to make clandestine contacts with the believers.

Try to learn a few words in their language, even if it's only "hello" and "goodby," and "God bless you." They'll love you for trying. Don't make comparisons between our country and theirs unless it is positive. Keep off of political subjects; speak rather about the Lord. Avoid using phrases like "the free world" and "the Iron Curtain."

Keep in mind that they have problems we have never dreamed of. Try not to add to their difficulties by attracting attention to yourself either by dress or behavior. We can leave their country - - they cannot! Caution and precaution may make the difference between a memorable trip and a nightmare.

Bill Bathman

* * * * * * *

Perhaps I could just list some important points for travelers to remember. It's important to keep in mind that each country in Eastern Europe differs from the others in the way communism is administered. And while a certain country may be applying a very hard line this month, it might have softened consider ably by next month. But here's my list:

1. It is unwise to take names and addresses of believers with you. They should be memorized. We used to suggest that if people couldn't remember the foreign names and addresses they could write the person's name between the lines of a favorite passage of scripture in their own Bible and the address in some other passage. However, if border guards see even an English language Bible or New Testament, this sometimes triggers them to search the vehicle and luggage more thoroughly for other literature.

2. There are standard questions on visa application forms, no matter which country you're visiting. "Purpose of journey" should be "tourism." "Destination within the country" should be answered by putting the name of a large city or town. NEVER answer this question by giving the name and address of a believer. If the form asks specifically for an address within the country (as the Czecho-slovak ones do), simply put "camping" or "hotel." If you are required to give your occupation on the visa application form, be honest - - although we would advise students not to put "student" unless they can't honestly put anything else. The communists are not great admirers of our Western students, generally speaking. Under no circumstances put down "missionary" or "minister of re-ligion." If you have no other legitimate profession, put down "teacher." After all, Jesus told his followers to go into all the world and teach all nations.

3. When arriving at the border, you might find that if you have any magazines, newspapers or books they will be confiscated - - this might be regarded as propaganda.

4. Keep your passport with you at all times. This does not mean putting it into your hip pocket or shirt pocket where it can be "lifted." Your passport is your "life-line" while you're away from home; to lose it is a very serious matter. And if you lose it in a communist country, no one will believe your story. They've heard it too many times before. Ill informed Westerners are often tricked into selling their passports to people who desperately want to get to the West. They (the westerners) are under the mistaken impression that all they need to do is wait for a couple of days before going to report the "loss" and all will be well. There are people in jail in Eastern Europe right now who fell for this con-line.

5. Don't be tempted to change money with individuals on the street or in public buildings, however tempting their rate of exchange.

6. Photographers should take more than enough film with them. The known brand films are not usually available in Eastern Europe, and if they are they're very expensive. When you've finished a roll of film, seal it up in the box just as though it hadn't been used. Do this especially if you have taken pictures of believers. Always ask for permission before taking photographs of individuals or congregations.

7. When visiting believers, try to blend into their culture and customs. Men never stand or walk around with their hands in their pockets. Ladies usually have their heads covered in church (although this isn't true in all countries). They wear dresses about knee length and with sleeves, or else a sweater. They do not wear a lot of jewelry or makeup. In most East European countries the Christian women do not wear trousers or shorts.

8. It's a good idea to have a supply of inexpensive ball-point pens, chewing gum, safety razor blades, toiletries, perfumes, etc., to leave in homes you might visit.

9. Insist on a full explanation of everything that is not clear to you when dealing with Eastern European tourist offices. If something is questionable, check and double check. This applies to prices, schedules, times of departure, etc. Every tourist office has personnel who speak more than one foreign language, so you should be able to find someone to speak English. BEWARE, even if officials say they don't speak your language, they might!

10. When you're with believers, handle your Bible reverently; do not bend or strike it. Don't put it behind your back. Don't make comparisons between your country and theirs unless it's to praise them. Keep strictly away from politics in any conversation; speak rather with them about your experience of the Lord. But don't refer to them as the persecuted, suffering church, or mention the Iron Curtain. Remember that these people were getting on with the job of reaching their own people for Christ before you arrived. Don't imagine that you have the answers to solve their complex problems. Your purpose for being there should be to learn from them.

11. If possible, learn a few words in their language, even if it's only "hello," "Good evening" or "God bless you." They'll love you for trying.

12. If you don't speak the language of the country you're visiting, you'll have to speak through an interpreter if you have the opportunity to speak in a meeting (not legally allowed in many countries of Eastern Europe). To make it easier for him, speak very distinctly, don't use colloquialisms or cliches, and use short, complete sentences so that he can get the whole meaning.

13. The Christians in Eastern Europe greet each other with a holy kiss. (That is, men kiss men and women kiss women - ed.) This may be a new experience for you, but it is a very precious and touching experience; not one to be taken lightly.

14. If you're invited into a home for a meal, be prepared to eat and drink e v e r y t h i n g that's set before you. However, we would recommend that you not drink the water; it might upset your tummy.

(name withheld)

HOW TO GET INFORMATION ABOUT CHRISTIANITY IN EAST EUROPE

> Beeson, Trevor DISCRETION AND VALOR Collins/Fontana, 1974. ($2.25 in Canada)
>
> "The present book, written by one of Britain's leading journalists, is the first-ever comprehensive report of the religious situation (in Eastern Europe). Material has been gathered and sifted by a team of experts set up by the British Council of Churches, and covers Russia, Poland, East Germany, Czechoslovakia, Hungaria, Yugoslavia, Albania, Bulgaria and Romania. The result is authoritative and without propaganda, but it is not without deep feeling.   (from the back cover)

Hebly, J.A. PROTESTANTS IN RUSSIA Christian Journals, Ltd., Belfast
First English edition, 1976.
A history of evangelical Protestants in Russia up to and including the underground church of the present day.

Unfortunately, both of the above titles, which contain first rate and authoritative information, may not be available in the U.S. Your Christian bookstore can order them from Canadian distributors.

Vins, Georgi TESTAMENT FROM PRISON Cook, $2.50
This is the story of a present day Christian martyr in Russia. The manuscript for this book was entrusted to Michael Bordeaux, director of a remarkable organization located near London, England, called the Centre For the Study of Religion and Communism. (Keston College, Heartfield Rd., Keston, Kent BR2 6BA, England) The Centre produces regular bulletins on the Christian situation in East Europe.
A number of other books about Eastern European Christians or the condition of the church in the East have appeared in the last few years, including several titles by Michael Bordeaux. Many experts feel that increased awareness in the West may help to bring pressure to bear upon government authorities on both sides of the Iron Curtain and result in more freedom of religion in the East.

For an annual analysis of conditions in general in East Europe in every area of life, look in your local library for THE SOVIET UNION AND EASTERN EUROPE, published in August by the Stryker-Post Publications, 888 Seventeenth Street NW, Washington, D.C. 20006. Illustrated with photos, graphs, etc.

8. Ethics For Travelers

Any Christian in full time work overseas values contact with praying friends at home. It is, in fact, his or her lifeline, both spiritually and financially. When, upon occasion, a valued friend from home is able to pay a visit to the missionary in Europe, it is a joyful occurrance for both of them. The missionary naturally does his best to entertain his guest (or guests), and to give that person a good look at the work that he is doing. He does this even though it is costly to him in time - - time that he often needs desperately - - and also in money (which is never in abundance). But, after all, giving is what the Body of Christ is all about.

However, most missionaries in Europe have a special problem because, being located in the most popular tourist area in the world, they find themselves having to cope with hordes of visitors each year. Knowing this to be a subject of general concern among missionaries in Europe who often are reluctant to say anything publicly for fear of giving offense, I asked a missionary friend in France to write down some thoughts for this chapter. He, in turn, consulted with some others. The following is the result of contributions from three missionary couples representing different organizations:

a. Don't presume your visit is always convenient.

   i. Often missionaries have to do a lot of entertaining in the course of their work and need to limit the number of tourists they can accommodate. We often receive other missionaries who are passing through, saving them the cost of hotels and sharing ideas and fellowship. There are also national workers and believers we need to help and encourage by offering hospitality.

   ii. In high tourist areas, missionaries are often overwhelmed by Christian tourists. Friends working with (blank) in Paris made it a point of spending the entire summer in camp work and other activities, confessing that this was the only way to avoid playing host to swarms of visitors who felt entitled to hospitality.

iii. Although it may not be obvious to the casual visitor, missionaries have a demanding work schedule so that sometimes extra people in the home can be a real hindrance to the work. On occasion the husband may be away on a mission or business trip and the wife reluctant to take in guests, especially young men, while he's away.

iv. Health factors are also to be considered. Sometimes the missionary or his wife are facing physical or emotional problems that would be compounded by the presence of uninvited visitors.

v. Consider also the living conditions of the missionary. Most workers in urban Europe have to live in small apartments and it is awkward to have guests sleeping in the living room for very long.

b. Recognize the job that the missionary is trying to do.
i. Whenever possible, contact him in advance to see if he can receive you. This is extremely helpful.

ii. Don't presume the missionary has the time to meet you at the station or airport and that he will be able to take day off to show you around town.

iii. Fit into his schedule. Don't expect him to fit into yours (after all, you a r e on vacation).

iv. Don't give his name and address to all your friends as a good place to stay in Rome or Paris.

c. Be aware of finances.
i. Be sensitive to how long you stay and the cost involved. The missionary's home is not just a free hotel. Sometimes he has difficulty providing food for his own family without catering to others.

ii. Remember, too, that with gas at nearly $2.00 per gallon, he has to count the cost every time he takes the car out of the garage.

iii. Phone calls are costly too, and toll free local calls don't exist in most of Europe.

iv. Don't presume that the missionary's faith should "carry" you too. Even a small contribution shows that you're not taking the hospitality for granted. A card or thank-you letter once you reach home is also appreciated.

d. Your attitude is important.
Have the attitude of a servant. Don't complain. Ask, rather, "How can I help?"

e. Be sensitive to the presence of nationals.

i. Language. One recent visitor became indignant because whenever there were nationals in the missionary home, the missionaries completely abandoned English.

ii. Food. Europeans don't live on burgers and shakes, and missionaries often adopt the national cuisine, especially if there are nationals at table. Eat what is provided without making an issue of it (e.g., horse flesh, snails, blood sausage, brain, etc.). A very poor family who had saved to buy their favorite dish for Christmas, oysters, were kind enough to bring them to share with (blank). An American student visiting (blank) was so expressive in her horror that people would actually eat such creatures that her inconsiderate rudeness almost undid a year's work with the French family.

iii. Drink. Respect your own conscience and refuse politely if you wish. Most Europeans will accept your convictions, though you should be prepared for a little joke about the funny ideas of American evangelicals. Don't make an issue out of it, and don't impose your convictions on others, including the missionaries.

help!

Find an error in this book? Get a bum steer? Know of some place or event that should be listed? In touch with a service project that needs volunteers? Don't just grind your teeth or throw the book on the floor and stomp on it. Write and tell us about it. The address is

Bob Baylis, The Pilgrimage Press, 2398 Telegraph Ave., Berkeley, California 94704

All contributions or corrections used in the next issue of EUROPE ON PURPOSE will be acknowledged .

SECTION B

THE
CHRISTIAN STUDENT

1. CHRISTIAN AND BIBLICAL STUDIES IN EUROPE

a. Bible Schools
     There are all sorts of Bible schools, Bible colleges and Bible institutes in
Europe, but most of them exist primarily to meet the needs of Europeans.
However, some do accept North Americans, and these are listed below. In
certain cases proficiency in a European language is a prerequisite, but most
are English speaking:
     Capernwray Fellowship of Torchbearer Schools. These feature short
     courses concentrating primarily on the Bible. For information write to
               The Registrar, Mr. L. Bert Burrows
               Capernwray Bible School,
               Capernwray Hall, Carnforth,
               Lancashire LA6 1AG, England
     Capernwray schools on the Continent are
               Holsby Brunn (some courses in Swedish, some in English)
               570-15 Holsbybrunn, Sweden

               Klostermuehle (German speaking)
               D-5409 Obernhof/Lahn, Germany

               Bodenseehof
               Ziegelstrasse 15,
               D-799 Friedrichshafen 2, Germany

b. Bible Colleges and Institutes
     A Bible college or institute offers a longer and more comprehensive course
than a Bible school. In most cases students may work toward a recognized
degree (this distinguishes a college from an institute). Missionary training is
an important emphasis:
     All Nations Christian College
     Easneye, Ware,
     Hertfordshire, England

     Belfast Bible College
     119 Marlborough Park So.,
     Belfast 9, North Ireland

     Bible College of Wales
     Derwen Fawr,
     Swansea, Glam., Wales

     Bible Training Institute
     64 Bothwell St.
     Glasgow C.2, Scotland

Birmingham Bible Institute
6 Pakenham Rd.,
Edgbaston, Birmingham 15, England

Institut Emmaus (French speaking)
  M. Frank Horton, Director
1806 St.-Légier, Switzerland
         This is a unique international missionary training school.
Frank Horton is an American and former IFES staff worker.

London Bible College
Green Lane, Northwood, MX, England

Moorlands Bible College
Sopley, Christchurch,
Hants. BH23 7AT, England

At the time that this book is being compiled there are plans afoot to start
a Regent College-type summer course in England. For further information,
write to Mr. David Baker, D.14 Peabody Estate, Wild St., London WC2, England
Send two international postal certificates to facilitate reply.

For information about accommodations in Bible schools and colleges during
vacations, write to the above schools directly, or to Greater Europe Mission
(which has a number of schools on the Continent) - address in section C.2.

c. Theological Training
    Graduate theological training in Britain and Europe is generally obtained
through the theology departments of regular universities (although there are a
few evangelical graduate schools of theology). The theological seminary concept
of North America has grown out of our separation of church and state, whereas
in Europe there is no such separation. Students also pursue graduate work in
Europe in other areas related to the Bible, such as archaeology, Near Eastern
languages, ethics, African studies and so forth. In various places there are
evangelical Christian scholars in these departments such as F.F.Bruce
(Manchester), Allen Millard (Liverpool), Donald Wiseman and J.N.D.Anderson
(London), Jacques Ellul (Bordeaux) and H.R.Rookmaaker (Amsterdam).
Presbyterian theologians often do graduate work at St. Andrews, Scotland.
Certain Biblical scholars are qualified to do graduate research at the Tyndale
Library at Cambridge. For information about European or British universities,
write to the institution itself or to the national travel bureaux, and check the
WHOLE WORLD HANDBOOK.
    Of interest to students hoping to study theology in Europe will be the news
that a recent conference (Sept., 1976) held at the new Louvain campus of the
Belgian Bible Institute resulted in the formation of a European Conference of

Evangelical Theologians. This is an outgrowth of the 1974 Congress on Evangelism held at Lausanne.

d. Schools of Evangelism
A school of evangelism with courses of various lengths is operated by Youth With A Mission. This includes classroom instruction and actual evangelism training. There are also foreign language courses. During April, May and June students make a trip through the Middle East to Israel. For details and an application form, write to YOUTH WITH A MISSION
D-8931 Hurlach 1,
Schloss Hurlach, West Germany

Another school stressing evangelism training is located in Switzerland near Zurich. For information, write to Roby R. Maharaj
Jungerschule,
Sonnenberg,
9428 Walzenhausen, Switzerland

2. LANGUAGE STUDY

For information about a linguistics course associated with Wycliffe Translators, write to
Summer Institute of Linguistics, Horsleys Green School, Stokenchurch,
High Wycombe, Bucks., England

Many European universities offer language courses for English speaking students. For information, write to the institution itself, to the national tourist bureaux or to the Council On International Educational Exchange,
777 United Nations Plaza, New York, NY 10017

A neat arrangement for learning the German language takes place in Salzburg, Austria, consisting of a combination of classes with tours and outside contacts with people. For information, write to the
Internationale Ferienkurse fur deutsche Sprache und Germanistik,
A-5020 Salzburg,
Franz-Josef-Strasse 19,
Austria

Another European organization specializing in foreign language teaching is the ILC (International Language Centres). They, too, have vacation programs and cultural courses in various countries. Write for information to the ILC, International House, 40 Shaftsbury Avenue, London W1V 8HJ.

3. THE CHRISTIAN IN A SECULAR UNIVERSITY

Large numbers of students from the U.S. and Canada including many
evangelical Christians go to Europe to study in the various universities there
each year. Some gain spiritually from this experience, and others drop out.
The difference is often made by whether or not the Christian student finds
fellowship with other believers on campus and puts his or her faith to work
through prayer, Bible study and witness.

There are in Britain and Europe some Christian organizations whose main
purpose is to encourage an active witness on secular campuses by bringing together European Christian students. They will also extend help and encouragement to North American students whenever possible.

The International Fellowship of Evangelical Students,
    Mr. Chua Wee Hian, Director,
10 College Road, Harrow, MX HA1 1BE, England   863-8688

The IFES is a coordinating body for a number of national evangelical
Christian movements throughout Europe and the whole world. Some of the
national movements such as the USCF (formerly IVF) in Britain, the SMD in
Germany and the VBS in Switzerland are well established, with many student
chapters and a national staff of workers. Others, like Austria, are in the
pioneer stage. The IFES is interested in encouraging visiting students to get
involved in witness in Europe. Write to the above address for information about
any particular country.

The IFES sponsors international conferences in August at Schloss
Mittersill in Austria and at Oak Hill College near London, and a Christmas
evangelistic conference at Mittersill. Several of the national student movements
also have various conferences.

Campus Crusade For Christ,
  Mr. Gordon Klenck, Director,
D-7850 Lorrach,
Schillerstrasse 2,
Germany   07621/80 20

Campus Crusade work was started in Europe in 1966 by two couples and
now has (as of Nov. 1976) 303 full time and associate staff, 230 of whom are
European nationals. Crusade materials, especially the Four Spiritual Laws,
have been translated into every European language. The Lay Institute For
Evangelism is held periodically in various parts of Europe, and the Agape
Movement was started in 1975 to send European professional and skilled
people into the Third World.

North American students in Europe may write to Campus Crusade at the
above address for information about obtaining materials in European languages
or making contact with Crusade staff at European universities.

Large numbers of English speaking art students study in Florence, Italy, and there are various activities for Christians coordinated by Ms. Cora Hogue. For information, write to Casa del Benvenutu, Via Ricosoli 55, 50122 Florence, Italy.

An organization that is directed primarily toward students in Christian colleges in the U.S. and Canada is
> Study Abroad Program of Christian Colleges (SAPOCC)
> The Kings College,
> Briarcliff Manor, NY 10510

This provides for Christian students the opportunity to live and study in various European countries "with other Christian students under Christian leadership and in close contact with Evangelical Christian groups and missions of that country." For details, write to the above address.

SECTION C
THE
CHRISTIAN MISSIONARY

Any Christian considering the possibilities of foreign missionary service should not overlook Europe. Despite the illusionary veneer of state church membership which results in statistics like "97% of the (Danish) people belong to the established Lutheran church," the truth is that the average European is a pagan materialist who knows nothing whatever about the Gospel. Churches for the most part are empty, public and private morality are degenerating, the cults and occult practices are flourishing and Marxism is the most popular philosophy in the universities. This section of EUROPE ON PURPOSE is designed to help you consider Europe as a mission field. It can also be used as reference by anyone interested in European Christian missions.

1. CHECKING OUT THE POSSIBILITIES

What are your aptitudes for missionary work? What sorts of opportunities are there for you to exercize your particular gifts as a missionary in Europe? What missions organizations are already working in Europe? There are the kinds of questions that need to be asked initially. Here are some places where you can get the answers:

INTERCRISTO, P.O. Box 9323, Seattle, WA 98104
For a small fee this organization will match your abilities and aptitudes with specific missions needs by computer. Write for the application form to the above address.

Short Terms Abroad, P.O. Box 575, Downers Grove, IL 60515
Upon your application, this service organization will send you a booklet entitled OPPORTUNITIES that lists short term missions openings all over the world. The book contains a form for obtaining further information from specific missions.

The Foreign Missions Fellowship, 233 Langdon, Madison, Wis. 53703
This organization is an arm of the Inter-Varsity Christian Fellowship, and is geared to helping students consider the mission field. Its most visible project is the gigantic Triennial Student Missionary Convention at Urbana, Illinois, but it also has various publications and services to offer. Most Christian colleges have FMF chapters.

MARC (Missions Advanced Research and Communications Center), 919 West Huntington Drive, Monrovia, CA 91016
For those wishing a complete listing of all U.S. and Canadian missions organizations (including those working in Europe), schools offering missions courses, plus a lot of other information relative to the subject of missions, MARC publishes a reference work called MISSIONS HANDBOOK. This should be in every church library. The 11th edition will be ready by the time you read this. It costs $15.00 postpaid, if you send your money in advance to the address above.

The William Carey Library, 533 Hermosa St. So. Pasadena,
CA 91030
   This organization stocks and also publishes a number of books relative to world missions. Write for a free list of publications. Particularly recommended: a 35¢ booklet called "The Two Structures of
God's Redemptive Mission" which helps to explain the history of
missions in Europe.

2. EVANGELICAL CHRISTIANITY IN EUROPE TODAY

What is the evangelical Christian "climate" in Europe? Here are some
ways to find out:
   MARC publishes "Country Profiles" on Finland, France, Greece, Norway,
   Portugol and Spain. They are 50¢ each. (Send for their publications order
   form. There are a number of other titles that could be of help to missions
   candidates.)

The FMF publishes a quarterly called MISSIONARY MANDATE which gives
up to date information about the mission fields of the world. Write for an
application blank for free subscription.

TEAM (The Evangelical Alliance Mission), Box 969, Wheaton, IL 60187,
circulates a free magazine about missions called WHEREVER, geared for
young people. Some articles are on Europe.

Harris, W. Stuart EYES ON EUROPE Hodder and Stoughton, London, 1970.
This is an excellent summary of the Christian background of each country
in Europe with the current situation as of 1970. Order from Mission To
Europe's Millions, 220-12A 8th Avenue SW, Calgary, Alberta T2P 1B3,
Canada. Inexpensive paperback.

Evans, Robert LET EUROPE HEAR Moody Press
Another summary of the evangelical Christian situation in Europe. This is
now out of print, but may be obtainable in libraries or from Greater
Europe Mission.

3. SHORT TERM MISSIONS OPENINGS

Want to go to Europe as a short term missionary (for a summer or a year
or two)? There are openings, provided that you qualify and can pay your own
way. By "qualify" I mean that you must be a reasonably mature Christian with
some history of having served the Lord here in this country, and you must be
emotionally stable. A person can't effectively help others if one is in need of
help himself, spiritually or psychologically. By "pay your own way" I mean air

fare and a certain amount for upkeep and daily expenses (this varies with the mission). You may be able to interest your church in helping to support you in this. Here are some missions organizations that are taking applications for 1977:

Bible Christian Union, Box 718, Lebanon, PA 17042
       Openings for college age young people in France, Italy and Germany. Can use both people with language ability and some without. Colporteurage, Gospel teams and camp work. Ask for the brochure, "Some 1977 Summer Overseas Missionaries To Europe."

Bible Club Movement, Inc., 237 Fairfield Avenue, Upper Darby, PA 19082
       or   Box 4052, Station D, Hamilton 53, Ontario
       Volunteers needed for work among children and young people in Great Britain, Ireland, Holland, Germany, Scandinavia, Italy and Spain. Language probably necessary for Continental countries.

Campus Crusade For Christ International, Arrowhead Springs, San Bernardino, CA 92415
       Office staff and au-pair girls (housekeepers) needed for short term work in Europe. Summer projects in Europe, mainly administrative work, are open to students and staff workers of Campus Crusade (Europeans are generally taking over field ministries). For further information, write to Mr. Don McDonald at the above address.

Child Evangelism Fellowship, Inc., Mr. Sam Doherty, Director, CEF Centre, Kilchzimmer, 4438 Langenbruck, Switzerland
       CEF can use both short and long term workers to do evangelistic work among children, teach them the Bible and also do some support service such as secretarial and bricklaying. "We have a desperate need for more workers all over Europe."

Christian Literature Crusade, P.O. Box C, Fort Washington, PA 19034
(See supplement at the end of A.6 for addresses of CLC stores in Europe.)
       CLC can use one or two couples in Italy for summer help even though not proficient in the language. Otherwise, they need only people who are fluent in German, French, Italian or Dutch and who have had some business experience.

Conservative Baptist Foreign Mission Society, P.O. Box 5, Wheaton, IL 60187
       The Missionary Assistance Corps (which offers all sorts of jobs, but mostly teaching and counseling) has some openings in Italy at present, and occasionally in other parts of Europe. Others besides Baptists may apply.

Dilaram Houses, Heidebeek, Heerde, Holland
The work of Dilaram Houses is "intense involvement in the lives of alienated young people through Christian community." There are summer openings for short term training in this ministry in Holland, Spain and England.

Eastern European Bible Mission, P.O. Box 1843, Regina, Sask. S4P 3El, Canada
This organization is affiliated with Brother Andrew, author of GOD'S SMUGGLER. There are openings for summer service "for certain individuals that God specifically calls to our ministry." Write for the brochure, "Answers".

Eurocorps-77, Greater Europe Mission, P.O. Box 668, Wheaton, IL 60187
Eurocorps is described as "a missionary venture in miniature." In summer 1977 about one hundred young people will become involved in Europe missions service, mainly in manual labor and support ministries. There will also be some evangelistic opportunities for those with language abilities. Ask for the brochure, "EUROCORPS 77".

Gospel Missionary Union, Smithville, MO 64089
Evangelistic campaigns and church planting work in France, Spain, Belgiam, Austria and Italy. Opportunities for two year service, which includes language training.

Operation Mobilization (Send the Light, Inc.), P.O. Box 148, Midland Park, NJ 07432
OM is primarily a literature evangelism movement stressing individual discipleship and community involvement on a team basis. There are opportunities for service in various parts of Europe (Belgium, France, Spain, Austria, Italy) for a summer, or up to two years or more. OM also operates the ship "Logos".

Overseas Christian Servicemen's Centers, P.O. Box 10308, Denver, CO 80210
The OCSC has six centers in Europe, each run by a couple assisted by Christian military personnel. There are some limited needs for summer help by skilled Bible teachers.

The Pocket Testament League, Inc., 117 Main St., P.O. Box 368, Lincoln Park, NJ 07035
The Pocket Testament League is basicly a literature distribution mission, though other kinds of ministries fall under its jurisdiction as well. There are various needs for short term workers ranging from helping with sound trucks to typing. Ask for the brochure, "Limited Term Possibilities with PTL."

Prince of Peace Corps - Global Outreach, Box 20905, Phoenix, Arix. 85036
        The "Prince of Peace Corps" is made up of young people who volunteer for a summer of evangelization in Europe through "music, literature, and crusades." Teams will go to Ireland, Holland, Germany and France. Write for the brochure called "Prince of Peace Corps Summer Program."

The Slavic Gospel Association, Inc., Box 1122, Wheaton, IL 60187
        For summer 1977 the Slavic Gospel Association has need for "Christians, college age and older, who can do evangelistic outreach and have discipleship ministries in northern France," and "mature Christians, college age and older, who are burdened for the Russian and Slavic people" for a literature distribution ministry in East Europe. There are openings for both foreign language speaking volunteers and support workers.

Student Training In Missions, Inter-Varsity Christian Fellowship, 233 Langdon, Madison, Wis. 53703
        Student Training In Missions consists of the opportunity for selected students from the U.S. to spend a summer working with missionaries in various parts of the world. The students receive a thorough training beforehand and also evaluate their experience. Open to students in IVCF chapters.

TEAM - The Evangelical Alliance Mission, P.O. Box 969. Wheaton, IL 60187
        The TEAM summer ministries include a wide variety of services - e.g., evangelism, camp work, radio technology, children's clubs, door to door visitation, secretaries, medical workers, English teachers, maintenance crews, youth workers, etc. The volunteers must match current needs. Direct ministries require a knowledge of the language, as usual. Openings now in France, Portugal and Austria.

Torchbearers - J.S.Burroughs, pasteur, "Chalet des Sept Bonheurs,"
Lot. La Pignada Qu. Martiénea, 64210 BIDART, France
        This lively work in the southwest of France can use two young men fluent in French for a youth evangelism and coffee house ministry, two young women (ditto on the French) to do youth work among teenagers and children, and one young man for practical work and maintenance. References and support required. Time of need is July 15-August 24, but there are possibilities for starting a year team.

United Beach Missions, P.O. Box H.P. 3, Leeds LS6 3BS, England
        This is a children's evangelistic ministry at Britain's various beach resorts that has flourished for many years. The programs are operated mainly by Christian university students or collage age young people.

Youth With A Mission, P.O. 1099, Sunland, CA 91040
> This organization, like OM, is community oriented and is directed toward young people. They offer a "Summer of Service Programme" consisting of discipleship training schools, schools of evangelism, evangelistic teams and special projects (such as evangelism at world fairs). Dilaram Houses (see above) are part of Youth With A Mission ministries. Write to the above address for details or to
Jeunesse en Mission, Case Postale 325, 1010 Lausanne, Switzerland

Youth Hostel Ministries, Wheaton College, Wheaton, IL 60187
> This is a unique witnessing operation involving teams that go the youth hostel circuit in Europe, making contact with the young people who stay at these places. Open only to Wheaton students.

4. NON-PROFESSIONAL MISSIONS

Some Christians have found a very effective ministry as "non-professional" missionaries, or Christian workers who get their support by working at secular jobs overseas. This is an area that has a great deal of potential, because many times a Christian employed in a profession has contact with a class of people whom missionaries cannot reach. A non-professional missionary can also give strong support to his full time or "professional" counterpart in a European community, especially if he or she has a good grasp of the language.

Practically nothing has been written about this type of missions approach, yet since the very early beginnings of modern Protestant missions non-professional missionaries were active, sometimes as military or company chaplains (as Henry Martyn), others as business people or teachers. If you are interested in this concept, some help and direction may be obtained through the Foreign Missions Fellowship or MARC. Research in preparation for a book on the subject is now being done by a Christian who has had many years of experience in this area, but it is not forthcoming in the immediate future.

Regarding getting a secular job in Europe, the best source of help at present is the WHOLE WORLD HANDBOOK (which lists various agencies) or one of the practical guides. (See Guidebook section beginning p. 123) Public libraries can also offer some help.